THE COMPLETE BOOK
OF DECOUPAGE

Revised Edition

THE COMPLETE BOOK OF DECOUPAGE

Frances S. Wing

A BERKLEY WINDHOVER BOOK
published by
BERKLEY PUBLISHING CORPORATION

Contents

Preface

Decoupage is forever. It's a decorative art which can be completely yours—or it can be a copy of someone else's design. Your copy may be even better than the original if your coloring, cutting, and finish are better. Without cutouts there can be no decoupage, the word being derived from the French *couper*—to cut. And without good design there can be no good decoupage. It is the art of decorating surfaces permanently with paper cutouts. And if you want a good piece of decoupage, you must use many cutouts and combine them to make a new, personalized design.

Since publication of this book in 1965 thousands who had never heard the word before have learned to do good decoupage. There are hundreds of new teachers and studios where you can learn the art or buy supplies. There are new products for the art, such as new glues, varnishes, lacquers, and gold-leaf size (see page 60). There are new groups working together to exchange ideas and to do decoupage for charity.

Despite all the new products, my personal recommendation for a finish is McCloskey's Heirloom Crystal Clear Gloss Finish, which yellows very little or McCloskey's Heirloom Flat, which yellows quite a lot.

One lacquer which I have found easy to use is Deft. This can be put on every hour with good results, provided you work where the atmosphere is dry. I use it for objects which are not handled frequently. The final finish is excellent.

As for glue, I have not found any which can touch Duratite, which can be used on wood or glass with equally good results.

Along with the increase of good teachers, new studios, and new products have come poor teachers and lots of decorative items which have no relationship to decoupage except a good finish. My theory is that the history of decoupage (Chapter 1) shows that originally the decorative art was called "poor man's lacquer" in Europe, and there was great emphasis on finish. This, I believe, is one reason so many today consider "decoupage" simply applying a good finish over anything from a beat-up board with a pasted picture to a paper-covered box with gold paper braid. I even read in one newspaper that decoupage was the finish itself. But "it ain't necessarily so."

My favorite term for the artsy-craftsy non-decoupage was given me by Vi Payne of Sarasota—a well-known decoupeur. She learned it from her five-year-old granddaughter who one day locked her mother out of the nursery. Her mother went about her business but in an hour came back and demanded to be admitted to the nursery. Rosy-cheeked Meggie opened the door, and her mother gazed upon a card table covered with ribbon, Christmas cards, cardboard, glue, and scissors.

"What in the world do you think you're doing?" she asked. "Oh, you know, Mom, what gram does, 'deckin' and podgin'.' "

There is a lot of deckin' and podgin' going on in this world. And when you hear that a so-called teacher will instruct 600 people at a time, you can be sure that all you'll learn will be just that—deckin' and podgin'. You'd be much better off to stay home and read a good book—this one, for example. Because this book was written for those who want to know how to practice decoupage properly.

Decoupage takes time and elbow grease in addition to a good color sense, nimble fingers, and a sense of design. But anyone who is willing either to study a good book or to study with a good teacher can learn the art. It's not reserved, as some would lead us to believe, for either the professional artist or the millionaire. Anyone—artist or layman, rich or poor, can do decoupage, provided there is the wish to do it and the will to learn to do it properly. This book will tell you what the art is and how to do it. The rest is up to you.

Part I

Frontispiece. Venetian secretary—latter half of 18th century—owned by and on permanent display at the Ringling Museum of Art, Sarasota, Fla. The background color is ivory. The top and most of the raised portions are gold-leafed. The scrolls around the cutouts (trees, figures, etc.) are painted dark blue. The cutouts are in shades of brown, green, yellow, and blue.

I

What Is Decoupage?

"D ECOUPAGE" is a word adopted in the 20th century to describe the art of decorating surfaces permanently with paper cutouts. To all who know and love it, it is a word of magic. For some, it evokes enchanting pictures of 18th-century chinoiserie decorations. For others, it calls to mind all the delights of a modern studio where friends work together to create exquisitely decorated objects ranging from a simple box to a magnificent piece of furniture. A sense of color, knowledge of design, nimble fingers, and vast patience are required to produce a work of art in decoupage. But everyone, from a six-year-old to a nonagenarian, can master it in its simplest form.

Decoupage as it is practiced today is a revival of an art which flourished in 18th-century Europe. The word is French and comes from *"couper"*—to cut. But for some curious reason, French dictionaries do not define "decoupage" as a decorative art but as cutting out or stamping out leather and metal. Although the word has been used in this country since the early 1900's to refer to decorating with cutouts, it was not included in an American dictionary until 1961 when Webster's Third International Dictionary, Unabridged, 1961 (G. and C. Merriam Co., Springfield, Mass.), defined it as "1: The art of decorating surfaces with paper cut-outs . . ."

I define decoupage as "the Art of the Four C's—COLOR (Chapter 3); CUT (Chapter 4); CREATE (Chapter 5); and COVER (Chapters 6 and 7). The first step in decorating with cutouts is to select prints, or copies of them, and *color* them. The second step is to *cut* out the colored prints with care. The third step is to *create* a decorative design from the cutouts. And the final step is to *cover* the design with varnish or lacquer and rub it down to the soft satin-glow of antique furniture. Covering also includes working under glass where your cover is already provided for you, or working in shadow boxes which are again covered with glass.

It sounds simple, doesn't it? But even the simplest definitions are likely to be confusing if you've never seen a piece of decoupage. Take time out now to study the photographs in the latter half of the book and you will immediately understand exactly what decoupage is—remember that all the decorative designs you see are made from paper cutouts and are not painted on.

Decoupage is a decorative art and should be distinguished from such art forms as collage and montage. "Collage" comes from the French *"coller"*—to glue. Pablo Picasso is given credit for having first used this form in 1912 in his "Still Life with Chair Caning." The chair caning was a piece of oilcloth painted to look like caning and glued onto the canvas.

What Is Decoupage?

The picture was termed a collage and artists such as Georges Braque and Juan Gris joined Picasso in developing it as a revolt against slick brushwork and artificial techniques. It is widely practiced today and has come to mean a picture in which extraneous objects are included, such as bits of string, a real watch, fragments of wood, metal, shells, etc.

"Montage"—from the French *"monter"*—to mount—is frequently confused with collage. It is an older art form which began in the nineteenth century and was first done only with photographs and called photomontage. A collection of photographs was pasted on a surface in such a manner that the total effect was a new artistic production. Today, montages frequently include other flat forms, such as pictures cut or torn from a magazine or other source.

Both a collage and a montage may include cut-out figures. That is why they are often confused with decoupage. A picture done completely from cutouts may properly be called decoupage. But the inclusion of a few cutouts in a collage or montage does not transform these art forms to decoupage.

Plate No. 1 shows one of Carl Federer's delightful creations. It was done largely with cutouts and is referred to in *Craft Horizons* as decoupage (Mary Lyon, "The Lively Art of Decoupage," Summer 1950, p. 16). Mr. Federer works in all three art forms and is careful to differentiate each one. One of his pictures, for example, includes playing cards, dice, a watch chain, wire, a spoon, and a few cutouts. This he calls a collage—not decoupage.

The art of decoupage has an interesting history. The process was developed in the 18th century to imitate hand-painted Chinese and Japanese lacquer ware which was then so popular in Europe. Or, more precisely, when European craftsmen began to produce their own lacquer ware in imita-

Plate 1. *Carl Federer's picture from cutouts, courtesy* Craft
Horizons. *See text.*

tion of the painted, engraved, and gilded lacquers of China and Japan, some bright soul who wasn't adept at the art of painting came up with a new idea. He cut out the engravings of an original artist and used the cutouts to make a design on furniture which looked like painting after it was covered with coats of varnish. *Voilà* "decoupage." But not by that name.

Along the way, the art has been described as *"lacche povero"* (poor man's lacquer) and *"lacca contrafatta"* or *"lacca contrafacta"* (simulated lacquer) by the Italians; *"lacque pauvre"* (from the Italian) and *"l'art 'scriban'"* or *"l'art 'scribanne'"* (art of the desk) by the French; and "japanning" (lacquering) by the English.

Notice the prevalence of "lacquer" in these terms. This is because the art came into existence to imitate decorated lacquer ware. Long before decorating with paper cutouts came into vogue, Europeans were producing products which could be used to simulate Chinese and Japanese lacquers and to give a hard finish over painted wood and metal. The craze for Chinese and Japanese screens, boxes, fans, trinkets, vases, etc., was so universal that importers could not possibly meet the demand. Everyone who could afford it wanted a piece of Oriental lacquer. Decorated lacquer ware became a status symbol.

In the 17th century, European craftsmen did little more than copy designs from imported Oriental decorated lacquers. But in the 18th century a style of painting and of decorating, known as "chinoiserie" (a style showing the influence of Chinese art) came into vogue. Far from being a copy of Oriental art, this style was completely individualistic. The chinoiserie masterpieces of 18th-century European artists were created because the artists' imaginations were stirred by their "vision of Cathay." But the style remained uniquely European.

It was in this century with its interest in chinoiserie and the rococo that the art we now call decoupage first flowered. Although today's decoupeurs think of the art as essentially French because the word is French and many of the prints used today are copies of 18th-century French ones, the art apparently began in Italy.

Serge Roche, a Parisian dealer in antiques and an authority on Venetian lacquers, tells us that Venetian decorators of the 18th century evolved the idea of getting the effect of painted lacquer ware by using cut-out engravings which were pasted to painted wood and then lacquered ("Le Décor 'Scriban,'" *Plaisir de France*, Noël 1960, p. 77). After the process was invented, he adds, engravings were sometimes especially made for it, but many artisans searched for all types of engravings which could be combined in a new design. The result was that it was not unusual to find Italian engravings side by side with those of French and German engravings.

Other authorities agree with Mr. Roche that the art began in Italy. But no matter where it began, its popularity soon spread to France and many other European countries, including England. And there is no question that it was greatly influenced by 18th-century French artists and particularly by those working in the chinoiserie style. Of these, Huet, Boucher, Watteau and Pillement were the leading designers for 18th-century decorative art which has never been surpassed in beauty, elegance, and charm. And these artists have been the darlings of decoupeurs over the centuries.

Outstanding among the artists working in the chinoiserie

was Jean Pillement. His gay and witty drawings of dancing Chinese figures, of fragile bridges and houses swaying from exotic trees, of delicious hatted flowers, of birds and beasts from another world, were used to decorate walls, tapestries, silks, spinets, clocks, desks, screens, boxes, and trinkets. Engravings of his work were used for designs not only in France but in many other European countries, and today copies of his work are used by 20th-century decoupeurs to re-create the elegance and whimsy of the 18th century. No wonder Pillement is frequently referred to as the father of decoupage. But it is doubtful that he ever heard the word used to describe the art form we know today. In fact, he was so busy creating new designs that it's inconceivable that he had time to pay attention to minor artists and craftsmen who might be cutting up his engravings to use to imitate painting. Had he been aware of it, he probably would have agreed with Italian artists who gave the process the name "lacche povero."

Lacche povero—The most plausible explanation of how this term came into existence was given by Serge Roche who argues that the term was adopted because the original artists whose engravings were being cut up looked with scorn on their imitators. Not wishing to be associated in any way with the process, they called it "lacche povero"—or poor man's lacquer. The term would seem to be particularly appropriate at the end of the 18th century when the work began to deteriorate both in color and design. Certainly when we see examples of surviving work done when the art was at its best (see Frontispiece), we would not call it "poor" in any sense of the word. But in the days when lacche povero came into existence, top artists in all fields looked down on their helpers and on their imitators. Today, in Italy, the term for our decoupage is "lacca contrafatta" or "lacca contrafacta," meaning simulated lacquer.

L'art "scriban"—A second term used in the 18th century to designate decoupage—and still used in France today—is "l'art 'scriban'" or "l'art 'scribanne.'" This term is not so easily explained, but again M. Roche has an imaginative theory. "Scriban" means a desk with drawers. Today it has been replaced in common usage by "secrétaire" (secretary).

How, asks M. Roche, did a word meaning a piece of furniture come to be used to designate a lacquer technique? While awaiting an authoritative answer from the *Dictionnaire de L'Academie,* he suggests the following hypothesis. Some traveler, stopping in at an exhibit and seeing a beautiful desk decorated with cutouts, overheard it referred to as "scriban." He understood the term to refer to the decoration on the desk instead of the desk itself and henceforth described this type decoration as "l'art scriban." Little by little, the term came to be accepted as designating art form and is still used in France today instead of the word "decoupage."

Japanning—The Encyclopaedia Britannica, 1964, states that "japanning," as used in 18th-century England, "included all sorts of glossy decorations in wood, leather, tin, and papier-mâché which emulated the celebrated lacquer work of the Japanese." Many of the designs were copies of the Chinese rather than the Japanese but the word "japanning" was adopted because of the superiority of the Japanese lacquer itself over that of the Chinese. When cutouts began to be used, japanning referred to this type of decoration as well as to the other types.

The popularity of japanning in 18th-century England is revealed by a book published in 1760 which contains some 200 pages with copies of 1,500 prints suitable for use in designing. Entitled *Ladies' Amusement Book* it was first published for Robert Sayer at the Golden Buck, London. A facsimile of the book was published in 1959 by the Ceramic Book Co., Monmouthshire, Wales. In 18th-century England the book was used by craftsmen and artists for designing everything from tapestries to ceramics. But the very title makes it evident that one purpose of the book was to furnish the ladies of England with material for their absorbing pastime of decorating with paper cutouts.

Most examples of 18th-century decoupage which are still in existence are in private collections, but there are a few pieces in European and American museums. One example is on permanent display at the Ringling Art Museum in Sarasota, Florida. It is a large Italian secretary done in the latter half of the 18th century with both decoupage and hand painting (see Frontispiece).

The beginning decoupeur is likely to run for the nearest exit if someone suggests that he undertake such a complicated project, one which would obviously take months to complete. But decoupage is a flexible art, permitting the decoration of anything from a pair of shoes to a baby grand piano. And no one need tackle anything beyond his capabilities.

Today there are excellent decoupeurs who are creating such beautiful objects d'art that their finished pieces may well be numbered among the heirlooms of the future. In fact, some pieces are already in museums (see Caroline Duer, p. 20). Many of today's designs are as intricate as any 18th-century one. But 20th-century decoupeurs have an advantage over 18th-century ones since our modern methods of reproduction give us access to copies of prints from any period we wish.

And we have usable material in magazines, seed catalogs, calendars, advertising material, etc., for those who have no desire to create a work of art but want the fun of cutting out and making their own designs. In other words, decoupage can be as elegant and gay, as precious and precise, as 18th-century decorative art; it can be as exciting and diverse as the art of our own century; or it can be just for fun and fancy. That is why the interest in it has continued to grow since its present-day revival.

Renewed interest in decoupage began early in the 1900's. The late Caroline Duer, for example, began the art at that time. She was a perfectionist who gave us some of the most beautifully designed pieces in existence. Her students found her a hard taskmaster but loved her for the professional work she insisted they turn out. The high quality of her work and the perfection of her designs is attested to by the fact that some of her trays are in the Museum of the City of New York, wardrobe doors are at the Cooper Union in New York, and a cabinet is in the Brooklyn Museum.

Another master decoupeur is Carl Federer who has worked at decoupage for twenty-five years or more. He wields his scissors with the skill of a magician waving his magic wand. From bits of paper, cutouts from magazines, old prints, postcards, and cardboard, he can build an entrancing picture on any subject you name. His sense of humor is so warm that it shines through everything he does. In creating his pictures, Mr. Federer combines his decoupage with other materials. Most of his work is a combination of decoupage, montage, and collage (see p. 13 and Plate 1).

Maybelle Manning and her son, Hiram Manning, have without doubt been as instrumental in getting modern decoupeurs to work with style and good taste as any two persons in the country. Men and women from all over the United States and even from outside the country have converged on their charming Boston studio and gone away to do decoupage on their own and to interest others in the art.

In an article published in 1949 ("Decoupage: Hobby or Vice," *American Home,* January 1949, p. 26), Mrs. Manning tells us that she became an "addict" of decoupage when she, with young Hiram, visited the French family of one of her son's classmates. There, in a country town outside Paris, she found a houseful of decoupage. She reported that the family taught her decoupage—an art which they had been practicing for years. Certainly both the Mannings learned well and they have brought to decoupage their own gaiety and wit, their superb sense of design, and their love of 18th-century elegance. Examples of their work and of that of some of their students are shown in this book. They speak for themselves.

Interest in decoupage was given a boost in 1958 when the first book on the subject was published. Dorothy Harrower's *Decoupage—A Limitless World in Decoration* (M. Barrows and Co., New York, 1949) is an excellent reference book, containing not only beautiful photographs of decoupage but of collage, montage, and many other art and craft forms. The author has worked in all types of decoupage, has lectured on the subject, and has taught students in many cities over the country.

Despite the amazing growth in the number of American decoupeurs in the past five years, however, there are still many who are discouraged from learning the art because of the lack of written information on techniques and because so many myths have grown up around the subject. The two most persistent myths are that 1) the art is so expensive that only millionaires can do it, and 2) it is so difficult that only trained artists should tackle it.

The facts are that 1) the art can be as expensive or as reasonable as the individual wants to make it, and 2) anyone can do it.

But no one can do decoupage properly without knowing good techniques which, once learned, should be applied to every project, be it expensive or inexpensive, difficult or easy. Having mastered the techniques set forth in the following chapters, don't let anyone tell you what you should or should not do in decoupage. There is no more flexible or individual art in existence. The fact that each of us can produce a distinctive and unique piece constitutes the greatest appeal of the fascinating and marvelously rewarding art of decoupage.

2

Preparation for Decoupage

W HEN I WAS A LITTLE GIRL, my father was constantly pulling that old saw on me: "What's worth doing at all is worth doing well." Nothing infuriated me more. Born impatient, I spent my early youth acquiring bruises and broken bones trying to do everything anyone else did without learning how to do anything well.

How my father's words have haunted me since I took up decoupage. If you skip one detail or do any step poorly, the end product will show you up. Even before you begin the first of our basic steps, the object you are to decorate must be carefully selected and prepared. Furthermore, you should assemble your prints and your supplies before beginning.

Subjects for Decoupage

Objects suitable for decoupage are practically limitless. A beginner, however, should not undertake a piece of furniture which might take months to finish. The choice of a small object for a first project will insure speed in learning the entire process of decoupage. After that, it is largely practice and experimentation. A partial list of objects which you can decoupage is given below. The starred items are ones which would be easy for a beginner.

Boxes
    Pillboxes*
    Stamp boxes*
    Cigarette boxes*
    Handkerchief boxes*
    Glove boxes*
    Letter boxes*
    Card boxes*
    Jewel boxes
    Shadow boxes

Trays
    Cocktail trays (large)
    Cocktail trays (individual)*
    Coffee trays
    Tea trays

Bookends*

Tables
    End tables
    Cocktail tables (either solid wood or glass top)
    Dining room tables
    Bedside tables
    Occasional tables
    Nests of tables
    Card tables

WASTEBASKETS

DOOR FRAMES

WALL PANELS

CORNICES

BED HEADBOARDS

MIRRORS

BOUDOIR ACCESSORIES

URNS AND VASES

SERVICE PLATES

SCREENS

MANTELPIECES

FOOTSTOOLS

CABINETS

CHAIRS

CHESTS OF DRAWERS

DESKS

PIANOS

SHOES (Believe it or not, I've seen them)

LAMPS AND LAMPSHADES

BOOK COVERS*

You'll find that you will soon add to the list by discovering something you want to decoupage which has been omitted.

Finding Materials

Not too many years ago you needed either a spark of the pioneering spirit or the persistence of a master sleuth to track down prints suitable for decoupage. Today decoupage studios, many of which are local and do not advertise, can furnish you with copies of old and new prints which are reproduced especially for decoupage. These prints will be easier to use than any other material since they will all be the same thickness and will not need to be specially treated before they are used; they are black and white or gray and white and can be colored by you in harmonious colors; and the selection will be large enough so that you can find all the prints needed for a design in one place. For example, a studio carrying copies of old French flower prints will also carry borders which go with these prints. When you are on your own and search for cutout material, you may have to go to many places before collecting all the prints you need.

But the search can be exciting. Go into museums and see what copies of prints they have on sale. Ask if you can have copies made from some you find but which are not among those already copied. Search printshops. Go into bookshops, especially those which carry old books. Send for seed catalogs. Look through magazines with an eye for spotting usable material. Go to wallpaper supply houses and ask for their old sample books. Begin keeping a file of material you find.

Why, if all these sources of material are available, do most teachers use especially prepared copies of prints? First, and let's face it, the instructor (your author included) has a lot of money tied up in such prints and wants to sell them. But there are other important reasons for using them for teaching. Let's look at each source and see the difficulties for the beginner in each one. Copies of prints sold by most museums are usually more costly than prints sold in studios and nine times out of ten are much thicker. Thick prints are difficult to cut and are difficult to cover with varnish after you have cut them out and used them for a design. You can overcome the thickness by peeling the prints before you use them. Turn them over and wet the back with a sponge. Now carefully peel one layer at a time until you have reduced the print to the thickness you want. I find that vinegar on the sponge works better than water.

Some of the original prints which you find in a printshop can have the same disadvantage of those found in museums, but most of these are on good quality paper which is excellent for cutting. Such prints, however, are often too expensive for a beginner. And unless you know that your decoupage will be as beautiful as the original prints, it seems criminal to cut them up. You can have copies made from them and use your copies for cutting up. A large number of my own supply of prints were copied from originals found for me by friends who spent hours in European printshops.

When it comes to such sources as magazines and catalogs, the chief concern is whether the material on the other side of a picture you wish to use will show through when you glue on your cutout and varnish it. To determine whether this will happen, spray the back side with a good plastic spray. After the picture is dry, if you can see no shadows on the side you intend to use, it is safe to go ahead. In using colored cutouts from magazines, be sure that your entire design is in good color harmony (see Chapter 3). No matter what your source of material for cutting up, you will find it fun to hunt on your own. And the combining of materials from many sources into a good design is really creative. Some of the finest and most original decoupage I have seen was done by Alice H. Balterman of Cincinnati under her own name and under the name A. H. B. Decoupages. For years she had saved pictures, prints, old theatre programs, etc., and about eight years ago found decoupage a highly satisfactory way of utilizing them. She learned the procedure through trial and error. But a look at photographs of her work (Plates 33, 44, 50, 56, and 71) will show that she taught herself well and that she was an artist to begin with. Such persons should pay no attention to so-called "difficulties" inherent in any type material found. Gather it all in from the four corners and give us more of your decoupage.

When you begin to look for objects to decoupage, again your studios will give you the most complete line of boxes, trays, picture frames, and other items. For the beginner this source is probably the best. But learn to look for things wherever you go. Try auctions, secondhand stores, thrift shops, antique shops, gift shops, junk shops, lumber yards, cabinetmakers' shops, glass and mirror shops. The joy of finding something unusual and bringing it into a decoupage group will be worth all your effort and will soothe those tired feet.

Preparing an Object for Decoupage

Let us assume that as a beginner, you have chosen the inexpensive, wooden card box the bottom of which is shown in Figure 1. The box is 6″ by 4½″ by 2″ deep. It has a wooden lining in the bottom half over which the top fits. Remove the lining.

Examine the box for nicks, nail holes, gouges, etc. If you find any, fill them with one of the commercial plastic woods

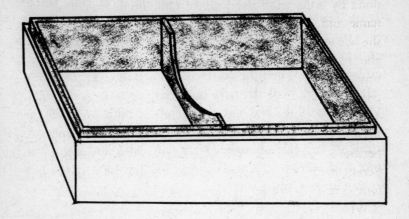

Fig. 1.   *Bottom of wooden card box to be covered with paper.*

or with wood putty, following the directions on the container. When the filler is dry and hard, sand the entire box,
using a 400 sandpaper if the box is very rough and a 600
sandpaper for a fairly smooth box. Finish sanding with 0000
steel wool. You will find that the best sandpapers are those
which can be used either wet or dry.

When the box is smooth, you may paint it, stain it, or
cover it with paper. Choose paint for your first project since
it is the quickest and easiest. Before painting, coat the box
with a sealer. There are commercial sealers on the market
today which are excellent. They can be rubbed down to a
flat finish and give a good base for paint. Ask your dealer to
recommend the proper sealer for the type paint you plan to
use—that is, oil base, water base, enamel, etc. Or you may use
a sealer consisting of one part shellac and one part denatured
alcohol. Drying time for commercial sealers will be given

on the container. It takes shellac about an hour to dry if you are working in a warm, dry place. Living in Florida, where the atmosphere is likely to be high in humidity, I work only in a heated or air-conditioned room. The ideal temperature is 70 degrees. Apply your sealer with a brush and let it dry. When the sealer is completely dry, rub down with 000 steel wool. Usually one coat of sealer is sufficient but if you find the box not completely smooth, wipe off the steel wool well with a lintless cloth (old nylon stockings are excellent) and put on another coat of sealer and again rub down with steel wool when the sealer is dry. Be sure the box is clean before you paint it.

PAINTING If you want some fun, ask a group of decoupeurs whether you should use a flat, oil-base paint, an enamel, or a water-base paint. Five will get you ten that the argument you start will still be going on when you steal quietly out of the room. My experience shows that it does not matter which type paint you use under varnish so long as you observe two basic rules. If you use a water-base paint, particularly on raw wood, seal the surface first with a commercial sealer. Second, after using any type paint, seal the paint before applying your cutouts, using either a plastic spray or a solution of one-half denatured alcohol and one-half shellac.

Personally, I prefer the oil-base paints because I like odd colors and it is easier for me to work with oils than with dry pigments or watercolors. There is no reason, however, why you cannot use enamels or water-base paints and get any color you desire by adding the proper color pigments. Ask your dealer to recommend the pigments.

Assume you choose an oil-base flat white paint, which will

turn a lovely ivory under varnish. Stir the paint well and, if the paint is thick, thin it with turpentine or mineral spirits. Several coats of thin paint are better than one coat of thick paint since thin paint goes on more easily and brush marks are less likely to show. It is not possible for me to give you the exact amount of thinner to put into a paint since paints vary so much in thickness. I like my paint about the consistency of thin cream but you may find some other consistency better for you. Experiment until you get the paint so that it flows on easily.

The choice of paintbrush is again an individual one. So long as the brush is clean and not too large, it will do a good job. I buy medium-priced brushes and throw them away when they begin to shed. And I never interchange a paintbrush with a shellac brush or a varnish brush. For small boxes, use a one-inch or one-half-inch brush. Brush the paint onto the box hard, going in one direction with the grain of the wood. Begin at the center and let your brush go over the edge of the box with each stroke. This will reduce the likelihood of runs. Where possible, paint on a horizontal surface. For example, begin with the top of your box and paint that first. Then turn the box so that one side is horizontal and paint that. Continue until the entire box is painted. When the paint is dry, examine to see whether the paint has covered and is smooth. If a second coat is needed, sand lightly with 600 sandpaper and repaint. That's all there is to it. Your box is now ready for an application of a sealer before any design is glued on. You may use a good plastic spray, a recommended commercial sealer, or a solution of one part denatured alcohol and one part clear shellac.

STAINING If you prefer to stain raw wood, go to your

paint store and ask advice on the type stain to use. Follow the directions on the container. For an excellent book on painting and staining furniture, antiquing, etc., see George Grotz's *The Furniture Doctor*, Doubleday & Co., New York, 1962. In decoupage, you will find painting more satisfactory than staining.

USE OF GESSO   There may be times when you wish to cover the grain of the wood or to cover myriad imperfections in an object. For this purpose, use a commercial, ready-prepared gesso. It is a creamy, white substance which can be bought in art and craft supply houses. Stir the gesso before using and apply it with a brush, your fingers, a cloth, or a palette knife. When it begins to dry, you may wet your fingers and smooth it easily. After smoothing, let it dry rock hard and sand it, using 400 sandpaper and finishing with 0000 steel wool. If you need a second coat, seal the first coat with a solution of one part denatured alcohol and one part clear shellac. It is better to put on several thin coats than to try to cover with one thick one which is likely to be lumpy and require more sanding.

You may apply cutouts directly to a gessoed surface or you may paint it. If you plan to paint it anything but white, however, I advise coloring the gesso the color of the paint you plan to use. Directions for coloring gesso are on each can. The reason for using colored gesso under colored paints is that it will prevent white showing through your paint when you sand the paint.

REMOVING OLD FINISHES   If you plan to decorate an old piece of furniture or any other old item, begin by taking off the original finish. Use any good commercial paint, varnish, or lacquer remover, following the directions on the container. Unless you know what the original finish is, ask the advice of your paint dealer on which remover is best. When you have removed all the old finish, carefully wash off the surface and let it dry. You will find that, when using some removers, you must neutralize the effects of their "eating" action by wiping off with a specific agent. Again the directions on your container will tell you what to buy. When the surface is free of old paint, varnish, etc., and is clean, proceed as you would for new wood.

METAL SURFACES For metal surfaces, the procedure is similar to that for wood except that you may have to treat for rust before painting. Sand any rust spots with steel wool and apply a commercial rust remover, wiping or brushing it on. If one application does not remove the rust, sand again and repeat. When the surface is free of rust and smooth, apply a rust inhibitor which may be bought in paint stores either in spray cans or in a solution for brushing on. When the inhibitor has dried, sand lightly and you are ready to paint. Many rust inhibitors today come in colors and you may find just the color you want in the inhibitor which would eliminate the necessity of painting.

COVERING A BOX Instead of painting or staining an object, you may prefer to cover it with paper before decorating it with cutouts. Choose a plain gold or silver paper or one in some other plain color, since your design will be made with cutouts and you do not want any design in the paper to detract from your own design. In some of the illustrations we show you, however, we have used a fancy paper so that it is easy to differentiate between the box and the paper.

Chinese tea papers are excellent both for covering boxes and for lining them. But they must be given a protective coating before using since the gold and silver on the paper is thin and will peel off. Two good coatings are 1) a solution of one-half denatured alcohol and one-half shellac, 2) Barrier, a commercial plastic coating which comes either in spray cans or in bulk for brushing on, and 3) a new commercial sealer to be used under lacquer finishes (see Chapter 6). For Chinese tea papers, which are very thin, use several coats of sealer. One coat is usually sufficient for heavier papers. I prefer Barrier and use at least five coats on Chinese tea papers. One coat is usually sufficient for heavier papers.

Assume you are covering the card box in Figure 1, p. 29. The wood lining in the bottom of the box is removed and glued back in after the box has been covered. Both the lining and the inside of the top should be painted. Use either a color which harmonizes with the paper covering or one which gives you an interesting contrast.

Covering a box is not difficult. Don't waste expensive paper on your first attempt, however. Practice with a cardboard box and wrapping paper until you get the hang of it.

Figure 2 shows you how to measure the paper for covering the top of the box. For the width, place a tape measure at the point marked A (inside edge) and carry the tape around the outside to the point marked B. For our box this width measurement is 6½″. Get your length measurement in the same way, measuring from C to D, which is 8″.

Turn the fancy side of the paper down and, on the underside, draw and cut out a rectangle to fit your measurements,

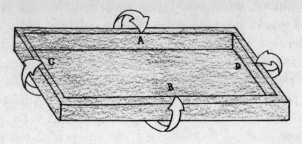

Fig. 2.   *How to measure paper for covering top of cardboard box shown in Fig. 1.*

which for our box are 8½″ by 6″. Place the box top upside down in the center of the rectangle and, with a rule, draw lines around the box and extend them to the edge of the rectangle by use of dotted lines. (See Figure 3.)

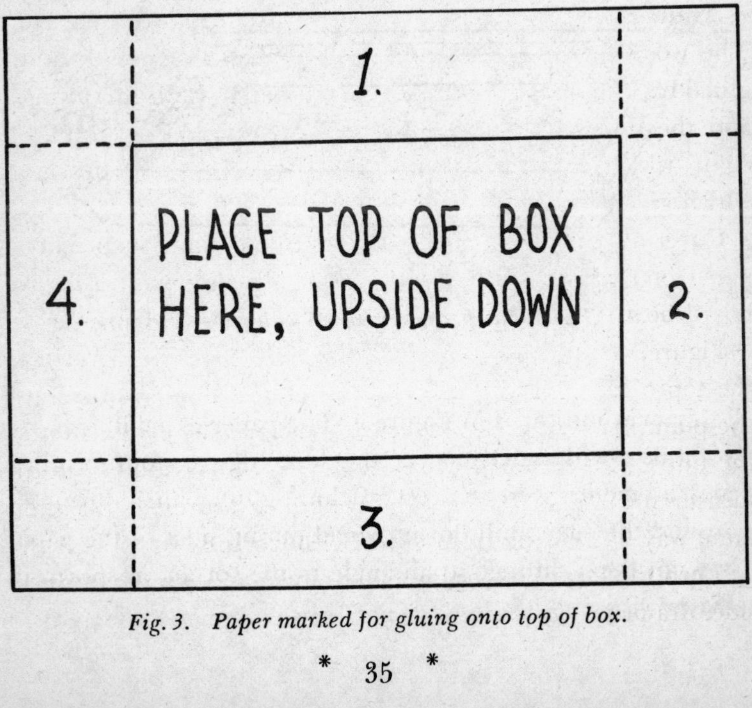

1.

4.   PLACE TOP OF BOX HERE, UPSIDE DOWN   *2.*

3.

Fig. 3.   *Paper marked for gluing onto top of box.*

For gluing, use a resin type, water-soluble, clear-drying glue. Pour a little glue into a small container and, with a brush, a small sponge, or your fingers, smear glue all over the outside top of the box until it is covered completely. Place in the exact center of the paper so that it fits into the solid lines shown in Figure 3. Turn the box over and smooth the paper, working from the center to the edges. When the paper is smooth, with no bubbles, let it dry a few minutes before gluing the sides.

Beginning with any side of the box, smear glue on it and pull your paper up tight and smooth. Continue around the box until it looks like the one in Figure 4. The folds at each corner come together on the dotted lines shown in Figure 3.

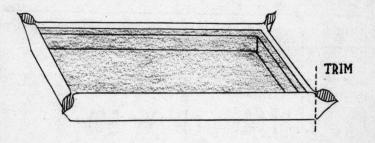

Fig. 4. Top of box partially covered with paper and ready for trimming.

Trim as indicated in Figure 4. The paper extending above your box will exactly cover the box edge if your original measurements were correct. Before gluing this down all around the edge, pull down two adjoining sides of the paper and cut them through at an angle in the corner, as shown in Figure 5.

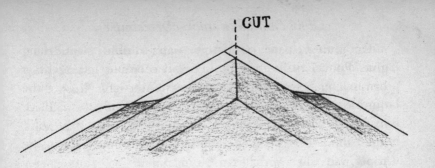

Fig. 5. *How to get a mitered corner when covering box with paper.*

The angle cut gives you a neat mitered corner. To cover the bottom of the box, place your tape measure at one corner and carry it around all four sides until it meets your starting point. Add one-half inch to this and mark it down as your length measure, which for our box will be $21\frac{1}{2}''$. For the width, measure is that between A and B in Figure 6. This measurement is $1\frac{1}{4}''$.

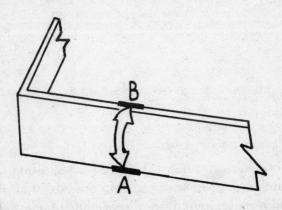

Fig. 6. *How to measure for width of paper to cover bottom of box.*

Cut a piece of paper to fit these measurements. Glue the paper to the box, beginning at one corner but letting the paper extend beyond the corner one-quarter inch. Keep the bottom edge of the paper exactly at the bottom edge of the box. When you finish, you will have ¼″ paper extending beyond the last corner. (See Figure 7.) Glue this to the ¼″ you allowed when you began gluing on the strip of paper and trim as indicated.

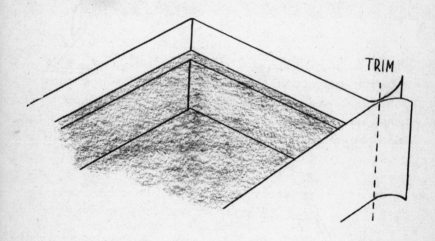

TRIM

Fig. 7. Bottom of box partially covered with paper and ready for trimming.

Since we were covering a box with a self-lining, we did not permit the paper to extend into the box at all since it might have interefered with a proper fit of the lining. If you are covering a hinged box, however, and intend to put in an inner lining of velvet, paper, or other material (see

p. 42 for directions on lining), your paper cover should extend slightly into the box. Figure 8 shows you how to measure for this. The width measure is from A to B and the length from C to D.

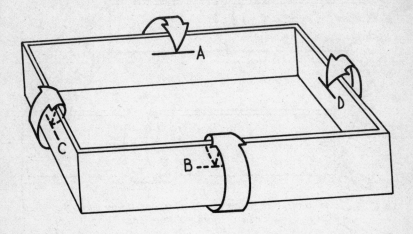

Fig. 8   How to measure paper for covering top of cardboard box if you want the paper to extend slightly inside box.

Or you may want to have your paper extend into the box so that it touches the bottom of the inside. Measure for this as shown in Figure 9 (from A to B for your width and from C to D for your length).

Remove your hinges before beginning to cover the box and proceed in the same manner as described above for covering a box with a removable wood lining. The only step which will be different will be the final one. Figure 10 and Plate 2 show you this procedure for the top of a box where

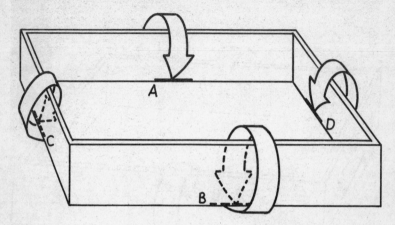

Fig. 9. How to measure paper for covering box if you want the paper to extend to inside bottom edge.

you want the paper to extend slightly inside. Figure 10 shows you how to cut the paper, first at an angle and then a straight cut. In making the straight cut, you are taking off a piece of paper equal to the width of the box edge. This will assure a smooth fit inside the box.

Plate 2 again shows the cut you make (see white line at upper left-hand corner of box). The right-hand corner of box shows two sides cut and ready for gluing down. The lower left-hand corner shows a finished corner.

Plate 2. *Top of box partially covered with fancy paper. Top left-hand corner shows white line indicating how to make a final cut before pulling paper inside box and gluing. Top right-hand corner shows how the paper looks after the cuts have been made. Lower left-hand corner shows paper glued down.*

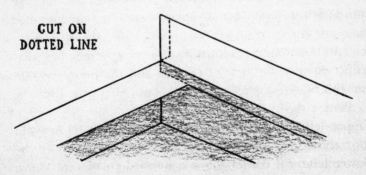

CUT ON DOTTED LINE

Fig. 10. *How to get mitered corner when paper cover extends into inside of box.*

To cover the bottom of a hinged box where you want the paper to extend into the box, proceed exactly as you did for the box with its own wood lining but finish it as shown in Figure 10 and Plate 2.

If you want the paper cover to extend all the way inside the box (see Figure 9), finish the inside by cutting a piece of your paper to fit the inside bottom of the box and glue this in after you have finished the covering. This will give you a box covered and lined with the same material.

For the sake of simplification, one step in covering a hinged box was omitted. What do you do about replacing the hinges? Plate 3 shows you a hinge placed on the left-hand side. Cut around it with an X-acto knife. On the right-hand side you can see the cut made where the hinge will be replaced.

How to Line a Box Many boxes are enhanced by lining them with velvet, moiré, silk, etc. This is especially true of jewel boxes. You will get the most professional-looking linings if you put your linings on cardboard.

Instructions for lining are included here because it is well to take the measurement for your cardboard pieces before beginning your decoupage design. Do not put your lining in before the box is completely lacquered or varnished, however. And if you are varnishing the box, remember that varnish changes the color of the box and the design so that your choice of color for a lining should be made after the box is varnished.

Figure 11 shows you how to measure for a lining to go in an octagonal box. This is the bottom of the box but the measurements for the top are taken in exactly the same way.

Plate 3. Box top partially covered with paper. When covering a hinged box, cut out the paper over the hinge before gluing to the inside of the box. Place hinge on the paper, as shown on top right, and cut hole the size of the hinge. Left space shows where cut was made.

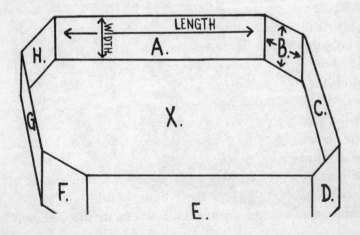

Fig. 11. How to measure for lining box.

The width measurement is the same for each piece. The length measurements are taken as shown by horizontal lines with arrows. For the pieces A through H, cut eight pieces of cardboard according to your measurements and mark each piece with the appropriate letter. To get your cardboard to fit into the bottom of the box (X), place the box on a piece of cardboard and draw around it with a pencil or pen. Now, take the measurement of the width of the box edge, which will be the difference between the outside measurement and the inside measurement of the bottom of your box. Take this much ($\frac{1}{4}''$) off each side of your octagonal and you will have a piece of cardboard which will fit into the bottom of the box. Mark this X.

Plate 4. Cardboard cut out for lining and laid on velvet. Dotted lines show where cuts should be made.

Plate 4 shows you how to lay the cardboard pieces on your lining material. We have chosen velvet. Place the material with the velvet side down. Now place your pieces of cardboard as shown in the photograph, with the letters showing where each piece fits toward you. Glue each piece to the material and cut on the dotted lines. You will notice that the bottom piece, marked X, is cut exactly the size of the cardboard pattern. For A through H, however, there is a piece of velvet extending beyond the top of each piece of cardboard. Pull this down over the cardboard and glue it down. (See Figure 12.)

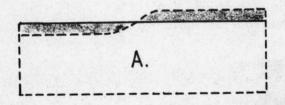

Fig. 12. Cardboard for lining, with velvet glued on opposite side and partially turned over for gluing.

Now when you glue each piece into the box, you will have a rolled edge at the top. Before gluing in, try each piece for fit. Because of the thickness of the cardboard and velvet at the bottom of the box, your side pieces may need trimming from the bottom before being glued in. When you have tested each piece for fit, glue in the bottom piece (X) first and glue each side piece in, beginning with A and going around until the lining is all in.

SUPPLIES

As you work in decoupage, you will find yourself adding to your original supplies. Below are supplies I use in my studio. The first list is basic. You cannot do a piece of flat decoupage without this list. The second list is optional. What you use of it will depend on how you work, how much work you have done for you outside your studio, etc.

BASIC LIST
Color pencils or other coloring media
Scissors, curved
Glue
Containers for glue and for water
Small brush for gluing
Sponge
Lintless cloth
Tape measure
Ruler
Varnish or lacquer
Brush for varnishing
Turpentine or mineral spirits
Sealer
Sandpaper
Steel wool
Wax or finishing compound

OPTIONAL LIST
A few cans of oil-base paint
Oil paints in tubes
Rust remover
Wood filler

Gesso
Plastic spray
Straight scissors
X-acto knife
Razor blades
Palette knife
Paper braids
Fancy papers
Gold leaf
Treasure Gold
Mother-of-pearl leaves
Velvets, moiré or other lining materials
Modeling tools
A tool for pressing down edges of glued-on cutouts
Denatured alcohol
Shellac
Pencil sharpener
Vinegar
Glycerine
Kleenex
Electric blender
Base tape
Cardboard
Chalk in several colors

3

Coloring Backgrounds
and Prints

ONE OF THE MOST EXCITING ASPECTS of decoupage is color.
Designs in black and white are always good, but there
is no step in decoupage which is more fun than coloring.

Many would-be decoupeurs come to me and say "Teach
me color." Immediately a scene flashes before my eyes of a
class in oil painting which I was attending for the exact
purpose of learning more about color. The instructor had
arranged a setup from which we were to do a still life and
had told us what colors to put out on our palette. "Go to
work," she said. "Mix the colors you see in the setup or mix
them to get what you would like to see." All except one
student went to work, as directed. The exception just sat
and finally announced: "I want to know what colors to mix
with what other colors to get the color I want."

And that's what most of us really want when we first begin to mix our own color. But it's not that simple. No two persons see color in exactly the same way. And the same person might see a blue, for example, as one shade from one angle and as another shade from a different angle. This is because color is reflected light. If a green box is in direct light from one side and in shadow on the other side, the two sides will appear to be different shades of green. And the green box will appear one color if placed on a red background, a different one if placed on a yellow background or a blue background. Furthermore individual taste in color depends on background and environment, on education, on emotional reaction. So color cannot be taught. But the student of color can be helped to teach himself by learning a few simple principles. The principles set forth below have been purposely oversimplified.

PRINCIPLES OF COLOR

Let us start with the primary pigment colors, which are red, blue, and yellow. By adding white to any one of these we can get innumerable tints of each color. For example, depending on the amount of white we add to red, we can get tints ranging from a red just a bit lighter than our original red down to a pale pink.

If we add black to our original colors, we get a darker shade of the original color. In practice, the addition of raw umber or some other dark earth color will give a shade less dull than the addition of black which, like white, is a "no-color." Or we can mix our original three primaries. Red and yellow will give us orange. Red and blue will give us violet. And yellow and blue will give us green. Figure 13

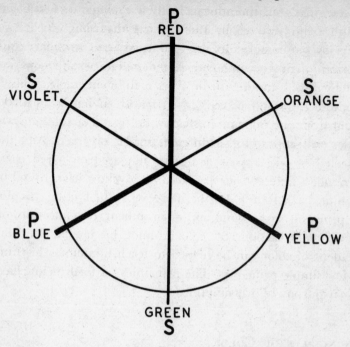

Fig. 13. Color circle showing primary and secondary colors.

shows these colors with lines drawn between red and green, between yellow and violet, and between blue and orange.

The primary colors are marked "P" and the secondary colors "S." The two colors at the end of each line are complementary and a mixture of complementaries in equal proportions will give you a gray or neutral color. An easy way to remember which colors are complementary is to think of Christmas colors (red and green) and Easter colors (yellow and violet). The two left are orange and blue.

If, instead of mixing complementaries in equal proportions, you add a small amount of one complementary to the other, you dull the other color. For example, you can get a dull, or grayed, red by adding a bit of green to it.

Now suppose we mix red with its adjacent secondary color, orange. What do we get? A red-orange or an orange-red. This new color is called a tertiary. By mixing each of the other of our primaries and secondaries, we have six additional colors. Figure 14 shows you our enlarged circle with the tertiary colors added.

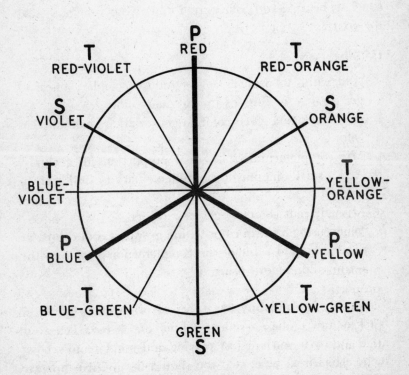

Fig. 14. Color circle showing primary, secondary, and tertiary colors.

To the right of the red-green line are your warm colors, those with yellow or orange in them. To the left of the line are your cool colors—those with violet or green in them. Notice that each warm color has a complementary color which is cool.

All your cool colors are harmonious and all your warm colors are harmonious. Suppose, for a note of contrast, you want to add a bright orange to a group of blues and blue-greens. Warm and cool colors juxtaposed are not harmonious. But if you add a bit of blue to the orange before putting it with your blues and blue-greens, you will have a pleasing contrast, because you have grayed down your orange so that the contrast is not jarring.

In Summary:

1. Add white to primary colors (or to secondary ones) to get a range of tints of the original color.
2. Add black to a given color to get a darker shade of that color.
3. Mix complementaries in equal proportions to get gray.
4. Add a small amount of a complementary to dull a given color.
5. Mix adjacent colors to get new colors.
6. When using a warm color with a group of cool colors, or vice versa, add a bit of the complementary color to the warm color before using it.

Now go out and buy five tubes of oil paint—a white, a black or raw umber, a yellow, a blue, and a red. Tell your art dealer that you are just playing and ask him to recommend which red, blue, etc., you should have. Oil paints are soluble in turpentine or mineral spirits so get a can of one of these. Go home and play until you see the wonderful array of colors you can obtain. But don't write me that you can go to a paint store and buy any shade you want because I already know that and that's what most of us do. However, you'll find that a basic knowledge of color will help you change a shade you already have on hand but are tired of using. And the only way I know for you to get that knowledge is to experiment, keeping in mind your basic principles.

BACKGROUND COLORS

Your choice of background colors for decoupage naturally depends on the colors in your own home or the colors in the home of your friend for whom you are doing a piece of decoupage. A natural wood color, black, and white are always good. White is particularly good with such styles as French Provincial, since it turns a lovely ivory under varnish. Black is effective with modern. But so are bright Chinese reds, yellow-greens, pumpkin, etc.

For boxes, screens, etc., try soft gray-greens, soft gray-blues, off-whites, Chinese yellows, or Chinese reds. But select your colors with the basic color principles in mind. And, when you choose a color, always bear in mind the fact that varnish yellows. A white, as we pointed out, will turn a soft ivory under many coats of varnish; an antique white, obtained by adding a bit of raw umber, burnt umber, raw sienna, burnt sienna, or yellow ochre, will turn a shade of yellow from pale to warm, depending on what was added to the white; a blue will become a green-blue, etc. Two-tone effects for your painted background are very effective for many pieces of decoupage. If you plan such a background, draw a pattern on the object lightly in pencil or chalk. An interesting two-tone effect is shown in Plate 5.

Plate 5. Italian box done by Mrs. Fred Sheehan, Louisville, Ky. The box is painted in apricot and white and the design, from Pillement cutouts, is in terra cotta, burnt orange, and ivory, with highlights of citrus-green.

The easiest way to paint such a pattern is to draw the pattern in lightly and paint in the light color first and the dark one next. In order to get a well-defined line between the two colors, you can use a small pointed brush and outline in the dark color around the light before painting in the rest of the darker shade. Notice that Mrs. Sheehan has separated the two colors by using a cut-out border which is fitted in beautifully and adds to the interest of her design.

Having decided on the color or colors you want, those of you who don't like to experiment may go to a good paint store, an art supply store, or a decoupage studio and ask for the color, tint, or shade you want. If you have a sample, take it and ask that it be matched. If you have not bought paint for a long time, you will be amazed at the number of tints and shades available. Every major paint company furnishes its outlets with specific formulas for mixing anywhere from 200 to 1,500 colors. And if you bring a sample which the formulas will not match exactly, you will find that the color specialist in the store will match it for you. You usually pay more for special paint mixes but it's worth it to get just what you want. When such formulas are worked out for you, the color specialist will put down the formula on the can so that you can go back for more at any time.

Many of my students, however, complain to me that they have to buy more paint than they need. The minimum quantity varies with different stores but few will mix less than a pint of a special color. The answer to this is to mix your own or to buy from decoupage studios, some of which sell paints in containers as small as 1 ounce. If you plan to try your own mixing, begin with soft tints, all of which require a lot of white. Get together the following supplies:

1 quart white, oil-base paint

A wide, one-pint glass container with a spout

Measuring spoons

1- and 2-oz. cups.

Wooden stirrers

Turpentine or mineral spirits

Oil colors in tubes. The minimum suggested are as follows: a cobalt blue (deep blue); a light yellow; a vermilion or alizarin crimson; yellow ochre; raw umber; burnt umber; raw sienna; burnt sienna; and Venetian red.

Small throwaway containers for mixing oil paints with turpentine. (I use metal cups which are 30¢ a dozen.)

1- and 2-oz. glass jars with tight-fitting screw tops for storing paint.

Before beginning to mix paint, thin your white (or any other basic color you are using) with mineral spirits or turpentine. The amount of thinner to use depends on the thickness of your white paint, which should be about the thickness of coffee cream. Mix your oils from the tubes with turpentine or mineral spirits before adding to the white. If you add oil paints directly to the white, the resulting color is likely to streak when applied.

Now let's see how we can change a can of paint by the use of small amounts of oil paint from our tubes:

Soft Yellow (gray-yellow)

1 cup white
1 T. light yellow
½ t. yellow ochre
tiny bit raw umber

Here we are lightening a yellow with white and then graying it with yellow-ochre and raw umber. Both yellow-ochre and raw umber are so-called earth colors and can be used to gray a color. Yellow-ochre is in itself a dull yellow and raw umber is a dark gray-brown.

Soft Yellow-Green

1 cup of white paint (oil base)
1 t. deep blue
1 t. light yellow

Here we are getting a soft tint of green (obtained from mixing the blue and yellow) by adding them to our white.

Soft Blue

1 cup white (oil base)

Add a tiny bit of deep blue until you get a shade you like. Try a touch of orange after you have mixed it. The amount of white you put together with the deep blue will bring you the tint you want. The orange, being complementary, will dull it so that you have a hint of gray in the blue.

French Blue

1 cup white
1 t. deep blue
1 t. light yellow
tiny bit of red

French blue is gray-blue. The blue in the white will produce a tint of blue, very pale. The yellow will give it a slight greenish tint and the deep red will gray it, since it is a complementary of green.

Soft Pink

1 cup white
Add vermilion or alizarin crimson until you get the shade you want. Add a little yellow for peach.

ANTIQUING

Sometimes you may want one of the antique finishes first used in the 18th century and becoming so popular today. Many of the major paint companies now put out kits with complete directions for obtaining these finishes. The kits contain an undercoat paint, a color glaze, brushes, sandpaper, and cheesecloth. The glazes which are wiped over the base color are transparent covers, such as varnish or lacquer, to which color has been added. You may make your own glazes if you wish.

Assume you want to do a box in antique white before applying your cutouts. Apply a base coat of white and let it dry. Now mix your glaze by dissolving some bronze powder in varnish. Bronze powders come in many shades of gold, bronze, silver, and color. Choose a soft gold. Brush the gold glaze over the entire surface of your box, doing only one side at a time, however. Let this become tacky and then wipe off the gold with a piece of cheesecloth until you get the effect you desire with the white showing through the gold. In wiping, use your cloth in long straight strokes. If your first effort does not suit you, wipe off the gold with turpentine and begin again.

If you are working on a carved surface, you may want to put your gold on first. Apply it only on the high spots and let dry. Then paint on a thin coat of white and rub off over the high spots until you have the amount of gold you want showing through.

These same processes may be used for any other color combinations or overlays you want.

There is a new product on the market which, to me, is even easier to use than the bronze powders. This is Treasure Gold, put out by Connoisseur Studio, Louisville, Ky., and sold today in many craft and art supply houses. It looks like gold wax and is put on by simply getting some on your fingers and rubbing on the surface where you need gold.

GOLD-LEAFING

And there is the more difficult process of gold-leafing. I once had a student who wanted to gold-leaf the inside of a lamp after she had applied her cutouts (see Chapter 7 for directions for lamp making). I suggested that we simply mix bronze powders and get the shade of gold she wanted because I did not think the final effect would be any better with gold leaf. "But," she replied, "gold leaf is what I want."

For those who want gold leaf and nothing but, it is suggested that you buy the leaves in booklets where each leaf adheres to a piece of paper the same size as the leaf of gold. The paper is used to pick up the leaf and comes off when the gold is applied to a varnished surface with pressure. The quality of your gold leafing will be determined by your ground, which must be glass smooth. If, for example, you intend to apply gold leaf to wood and the wood cannot be sanded to a satin finish, apply gesso (see Chapter 2) before you begin to lay your gold leaf. With gesso you can get as smooth a surface as you need.

When your surface is completely smooth, give it a coat of varnish and let the varnish get "tacky." Test with your fingers, and when the varnish seems to "click" you are ready. Take out a sheet of gold leaf, holding it on the paper side, and cut the size you want to apply. Press the gold side down into the varnish and lift the paper from it only after you have smoothed over the gold. If it cracked when you put it on, you can patch by putting another piece of gold leaf over the crack. Professionals, however, often work for an interesting pattern of cracks. Background colors for your gold leaf may be any you choose. Many of the old pieces had a background color of red earth. We can simulate this color today by mixing Venetian red and burnt sienna.

Gold leaf will not change color with age, weather, etc. But it can be protected by a coat of varnish. If you want to dull it, add a little raw umber to your varnish. Or you may get a ready-mixed egg tempera and add raw umber to this for a good, hard finish. If you find you enjoy mixing colors, don't confine yourself to a can of white paint plus a few oil colors. Buy other base paints and experiment.

(Since this book first appeared a new gold leaf size and a sealer in spray cans have been made available on the market. With the spray can size you can begin leafing within a few minutes by following instructions on the can. Two words of caution: Be sure your surface is glass-smooth before you put on the size, and spray in a thin film. If the size is too thick, it will not dry fast enough under your leaf, and this will cause the leaf to tarnish.)

Using Color Pencils

Background color is only one part of the color scheme; the second is the coloring of prints. The easiest and most effective way to color prints is to use color pencils, and the best are Derwent oil color pencils made by the Cumberland Pencil Co., Ltd. But there are good pencils made in this country, such as Eagle Pencil Company's "Prismatics." In learning to use color pencils, the quickest way is to use only one or two colors. This will teach you the importance of shading—or rather of emphasizing the shadings you find already on your black-and-white prints.

Plate 6 shows three prints. The two border prints are colored and the top part of the middle print, above the line, is colored. Notice how the shadings have been brought out in the colored parts. Suppose you are coloring the borders in two shades of blue. With a deep blue pencil, go over the outline. Hold your pencil at a very slight angle. I find it easier to pull the pencil toward me when outlining, but

Plate 6. Three copies of 18th-century prints. The borders, signed by John Ulrich, have been colored to bring out shadings. The center print (unsigned) is colored above the arrows.

practice to find the easiest way for you. Roll your pencil slightly as you work. This will keep your outline the same width. It is not necessary to outline every print but it tends to sharpen the design.

Next go over all the shaded areas lightly with the same deep blue pencil. Go in the direction of the lines which form your dark areas, or shadings. Do not press down on your pencil but hold it lightly and go back and forth quickly. Depth is acquired by repeated application of a pencil rather than by brute strength. When you have colored all the dark areas, take a very light blue pencil (silver-gray, which has blue in it, is excellent) and go over the light areas. If you want to lighten any of your dark areas, go over these also. Work from the dark areas toward the center of each light area. By leaving a little white, you can get nice highlights.

The tables in Plate 7 were designed from the prints in Plate 6. The borders and the leaves and stems in the large print were colored with a dark blue and a light blue pencil. The flowers were colored in soft pastels—yellows, blues, pinks, lavenders. The blues turned a soft yellow-green under varnish. Had I wanted a darker green, I should have used two shades of green instead of the blues. Remember that varnish yellows. In choosing your pencils, think of what yellow will do to the chosen color.

If you are afraid of selecting your own colors for a given print, try copying. Copy a print colored by your instructor or by a friend who is good at coloring. Copy a color print or copy a flower in a good seed catalog.

You are not interested in copying nature or copying others except to get you started. But try anything which will help build up your self-confidence.

Many of you, however, will want nothing to do with other people's ideas of color. I once had a ninety-year-old student whose chief hobby had been the study of wildflowers, ferns, berries, etc. She was fascinated by a black-and-white print of ferns and wanted to put the ferns in a lamp. She was horrified at my suggestion, however, that she color them in two shades of green. "Why," she exclaimed, "no fern has just two shades." And she proceeded to color the ferns, using three shades of brown, five shades of green, plus some blue and yellow. They were lovely and very realistic. If you are coloring

Plate 7. Three Italian tables done by the author from prints in Plate 6. The tables are a soft gray-green and the borders are a yellow-green. The center is in pastels with the leaves the same shade as the borders.

prints to go into a picture where you want reality, this is good. But if you are using them on wooden objects which will be varnished, you will get just as good effects by using fewer colors and concentrating on getting your shadings in properly. Remember that the better you get your shadings the more depth you will get in your finished product. Part of the three-dimensional quality of decoupage on wood comes from the proper shading of your prints. For the beginner, a few basic color schemes are usually helpful. Some are given at the end of this chapter, but you should work out your own color schemes which will fit into the décor of your own home or of that of the friend for whom you are doing a piece of decoupage.

When you get to the point where you strike out on your own and are experimenting with color effects, write down each pencil you use. It is too easy to forget what produced a particular shade and, if you find you need more prints than you have colored and cut, it is a simple matter to color more if you have kept a record of colors used. If you use numbered pencils, jot down on the edge of the print the numbers used for each part of a print. Before cutting the print, make a notation on a 3-by-5 card of the numbers used. Such a card might read as follows:

Print—Baroque flowers used for Jane's tray.
Colors—Roses colored with 1) Nos. 18, 16, and 72;
2) Nos. 21 and 18.
Purple tulip colored with Nos. 65 and 26.

In selecting your pencils, you may prefer to work with only a small number to start with. A good selection is as follows:

Cadmium, yellow light; cadmium, yellow deep; orange, light; orange, deep; a deep red on the blue side; a light red on the yellow side; a rose; a pale pink; a flesh; a dark, medium and light blue; three or four greens; raw umber; a medium brown; burnt sienna, burnt carmine; black and white; silver-gray (a blue-gray). Try out your pencils in various combinations. When you get an unusual shade which appeals, put down the combination used. Eventually, you will find that you automatically reach for the pencils you need for a given effect.

Some students prefer watercolors or casein to pencils for coloring. If you know either of the media, use them. But a good watercolorist is not likely to use watercolors on prints, because the papers on which the best prints are reproduced are not the proper quality for watercolor. If you insist, however, on trying watercolor and you know nothing about it, get a good watercolor book, such as *Whitaker on Watercolor,* Frederick Whitaker, N. A. Reinhold Publishing Corp., N. Y., or *Watercolor Painting—Step by Step,* Arthur L. Guptil, Watson-Guptil Publishing, Inc., New York, 1957, and read it through. You will learn from any good book on watercolor that you must mix your colors before you put them on paper. You cannot mix them on your prints because you will then get muddy effects. If you know nothing about mixing colors, go to your nearest hobby shop and buy a pamphlet on color mixing. A few basic instructions on mixing colors to obtain new ones are given under "Principles of Color" in this chapter.

Casein is used in a similar manner. But remember that casein is opaque unless thinned with large quantities of water, so that it is difficult to use without covering up your shadings. However, if you are adept at the use of casein, you can get some interesting effects by putting in your own shadings.

Suggested Color Combinations with Pencils

GOLD PRINTS

Sometimes you may want your prints gold. In order to keep your shadings, the best way to get gold is as follows: Select a bronze powder (available at art supply stores) in the shade gold you want and dissolve a small amount in turpentine or mineral spirits, adding a little varnish or solvent made especially for bronze powders. Keep your mixture thin. Experiment on a piece of paper to see whether you are getting the amount of gold you want. When your mixture suits you, apply it to the prints, brushing it on a small area quickly and immediately blotting it with a paper towel, paper napkin, or facial tissue. Examine to see whether you are getting the effect you want. The shadings of the print should show through. If you have an opaque effect, take off the gold with mineral spirits or turpentine. This process will have to be trial and error with a beginner but it is not difficult and is excellent under glass. One word of warning: Cut out your prints before you try this. The thin solution of gold will spread and it will be most difficult to cut out your prints if you gild the entire print before cutting.

Flowers

ROSES— Reds, yellows, pinks, whites, salmons
  For red roses, try a deep blue-red with a touch of purple, lavender, or blue over the deepest part of your shadings.

Highlight with light orange, yellow or white. Or use a bright red with flesh for highlights and a touch of deep red for shadows.

For yellow roses, use several shades of yellow with white for highlights.

For pink roses, use a soft pink or get this shade by overlaying white on red. Use deeper pink or red in your shadings. Use white for highlights.

For white roses, use a blue-gray or soft blue on your shaded areas. In working for a white effect, you may leave the white areas white or may go over them with a white pencil. The latter method is more effective under varnish.

Add a blue or lavender rose to a bunch of roses just for fun.

LILIES—Let your fancy run wild here.

Try orange with brown shadings and light yellow highlights.

Highlight a purple lily with light orange.

Use lavender or blue shadings on a white lily.

Shade a red lily with a deep gray. Add yellow highlights.

TULIPS—purples, reds, brownish red, yellows.

If you have only one purple pencil, try this over a green for a deep tone in your shadings.

For brownish reds, try a burnt umber overlaid with a deep vermilion.

For the tulip which, in life, looks almost black, try a dark brown with a purple overlay.

See yellow combinations under roses and daffodils.

LILACS—purples and white

Use purples, lavenders, and blues, particularly the gray-blues.

Try a bit of orange in your shadings.

For white lilacs, shade with gray-blue or lavender.

DAISIES—white and yellow

Use several shades of yellow in the centers. Use white on petals and shade them with blue, gray or lavender (on gray side).

DAFFODILS—yellow

Use dark, medium, and light yellows with white for highlights, and gray-blue or blue for shadings.

ZINNIAS—yellows, orange, red, rust, white, purple, lavender

See combinations under other flowers for all except orange.

Use bright orange with a touch of red in shadings and yellow for highlights. Or try purple or green in shadings.

Figures

A flesh-colored pencil is invaluable for figures. If you find yourself without one, try light red overlaid with light yellow and white. For highlights on flesh tones, use white. For shadings, try a touch of green or purple or burnt carmine and raw umber. For blond hair, use yellows with raw and burnt sienna. Highlight with white. Use a bit of purple in shadings. For black hair, add a touch of blue or purple. For brown hair, use several shades of brown, burnt sienna, burnt umber with red or orange highlights. For red hair, use burnt sienna with red or orange overlay. Yellow is good as a high-light.

Fruits

APPLES—Greens, yellows, and reds.

Use yellow highlights on red apples. Try blue in shadings, use blue highlights on green apples—shade with purple. Use reds for shadows on yellow apples.

BANANAS—Use two or three shades of yellow. Overlay part in white. Shade with violet.

LEMONS—Select a pale and a deep yellow. Try a blue or purple for shadings.

PEACHES—Try a light vermilion with a flesh overlay. Highlight with yellow and shade with burnt carmine.

ORANGES—Use orange and yellows with blue or lavender for shadows.

GRAPES—Purples, reds, blues, and greens.

Use a little orange for shadows on purples and highlight with white. Use violet for shadows with red and highlight with light yellow. Use green for shadows on blue grapes and highlight with white or light blue-gray. Use blue for shadows on green and highlight with white.

STRAWBERRIES—Bright red or deep red with light yellow for highlights and green for shadows.

Leaves, Grass, Ferns, etc.

Use many shades of green, combining yellow and blue-greens. If you have only a blue-green pencil, try a little yellow in light spots. Add browns and blues.

Borders

Bronzes, beiges, browns, golds, greens, deep blues, are all good. The color you select for your borders depends on your whole color scheme, including your background color. Highlight bronze with gold. Contrast beige with brown. Use two shades of blue or two shades of green, etc. To get a good gold under varnish—one which will look antique—first use a bronze and then a golden yellow on your borders. Touch up with a gold eyebrow pencil. The gold must go on last and the entire print covered with a sealer immediately, since the gold eyebrow pencil is likely to smear when put on paper.

4

How to Cut Your Prints

THE PRECISENESS WITH WHICH YOUR PRINTS ARE CUT will have much to do with the professional look of your finished work. Students ask me which step in decoupage is the most important. I do not know, since to me, one step is as important as another. But I do know that the cutting seems to be baffling to most beginners. And some never become beginners because they are convinced they cannot do the fine cutting which they have seen on a beautiful, finished piece of decoupage.

Yet, paper cutting begins in kindergarten and has been practiced since legendary times. Furthermore, it has been done in many countries with anything from knives to old kitchen scissors. Granted, the cutters were not working at decoupage, but much of the ancient cutting was the beginning of real art. In Poland, for example, women and children

—and sometimes, men—spent their long winter evenings cutting out brightly colored papers and fashioning trees, animals, flowers, and symbols. They made three-dimensional designs by building up layer after layer of cutouts. Their work was encouraged by the last king of Poland, Stanislaus Augustus Poniatowski, and is thought to have influenced later Polish art because of its preciseness. Other countries especially known for paper cutouts are Czechoslovakia, Germany, and Japan. Even today the Japanese use cutouts to decorate packages. And who among us never cut paper dolls or fashioned Christmas tree ornaments from cut-out paper?

Cutting in decoupage must be much more carefully done than cutting out paper dolls, but it certainly is much less difficult than some of the freehand cutting practiced by peoples all over the world. Get a pair of professional cuticle scissors with a curved blade which varies in thickness from a quarter inch at the widest part of the blade to the tinest fraction of an inch at the tip of the blade. A good overall length for the scissors is about three inches or a little longer. Revlon No. 2045, Miller's Forge No. 633, and Hoffritz No. 41/3¼ are three good scissors I have tried. Look at one of these and then buy a similar pair in a cutlery store, a department store, a drug store, an art store, a novelty store, or a decoupage studio.

Now tear something out of a magazine to practice cutting on. If you are right-handed, use your right hand only for holding the scissors and opening and closing the blades. (Left-handed persons reverse the process.) Use your left hand to feed the paper into the scissors and to guide your paper so that the scissors are cutting just on the line you want. Keep your paper well back into the scissors and use the tip ends of the blades only to cut into a corner before you turn the paper with your left hand.

One way to get the feel of proper cutting is to cut scallops on a piece of plain paper. With the paper held lightly in your left hand and placed into your opened scissors as far back as possible, turn the left hand toward the right and, at the same time, slowly close the scissors with the right hand until you have a half circle, or a scallop. Now move the left hand back and begin all over again. This is an exaggerated example of how the two hands should be used in cutting, but it is the easiest way I know to give you the feel of the proper way to cut.

The purpose of cutting in this way is to give you what is called a "feathered" look. After cutting out a print, turn it over and carefully examine the reverse side. You will see that the edges turn in toward the back of the print. This enables you to glue down your prints more firmly. If the edges turn up toward the side with the design, the job of gluing down is made harder. Another thing which feathered cutting seems to accomplish (why, I don't know) is to give a feeling of shadow to the pasted-down cutouts.

When you have mastered the technique of cutting scallops and have practiced on throwaway material, you are ready to try cutting a print. Before you begin, however, always spray the print (after it has been colored) with Barrier or brush it with a solution of one-half shellac and one-half denatured alcohol. Barrier is quicker and seems to give more body to the print so that when you cut fine pieces they are not likely to break.

Whether you cut the inside portions of a print first or cut the entire outside outline is up to you. It may be done either way. I prefer to cut out the inside portions first and, in fact, often cut the entire print as though all of it were inside cutting. If this makes no sense, look at Plate 8. The left-hand picture shows the print marked for cutting and the right-hand one shows the print cut out except for the bridges, which I marked to leave. The purpose of the bridges is to hold delicate portions firmly. And by leaving the outside

Plate 8. Copies of 18th-century prints. The left-hand copy is marked for cutting and the right-hand one is cut out.

edges of the paper on until I was ready to use the print, I was able to get more leverage in my left hand as I did the final cutting.

Plate 9 shows a picture of a print where the entire outside was cut before any of the inside was tackled. Notice the delicate tendrils on the outside. These are likely to be torn when you have to hold the outside of your cutout in order to do

Plate 9. Copies of a Jean Pillement print. The right-hand one shows the print cut out.

your inside cutting. Even when you cut the outside first, however, you will find the use of bridges of paper useful in cutting the inside portions. (See right-hand picture in Plate 9.) When you are ready to use the print, the bridges can be quickly cut away.

Many instructors tell beginners to cut a print into sections before beginning to cut the design. There is no reason why you cannot do this if it is easier for you. If you intend to use the print as a whole, however, it is easier to glue it on in one piece.

You cannot get the knack of cutting well without practice and more practice. But once you have mastered it, you will find it one of the most relaxing of pastimes. One of my friends tells me that if she has no cutting in the evening she is frantic because it is so relaxing that it helps her get ready for sleep.

5

Designing and Creating

T HE PLAINTIVE CRY "I can do everything in decoupage
except design" always puzzles me. Of course you can
design. Everyone of us is born with some creative ability.
The spark may have become banked with layers of self-
consciousness, lack of use, or just plain laziness, but it is
there. All you have to do is to encourage it. And there are
many ways to get help in building up your self-confidence.
Begin first by thinking of just what design is.

It is nothing more than selecting and arranging various
elements to produce a pleasing effect for the purpose at hand.
When you set a table, you choose your table linen, your
silver, your china, your crystal, and arrange your flowers with
care, but it never occurs to you that you are designing. When
you select the plans for your garden or patio, you may think
consciously of color combination, shapes of plants, where you

want mass, etc., but if you get a good overall effect, you have considered these subconsciously and have been designing. In fact, design is part of your everyday life. Good design is the best arrangement of various elements for the purpose at hand. And, whether it is good or bad, every time you select and put together items for a given effect, you are designing. I dislike talking good or bad design since it is so much a matter of personal taste. It not only involves the mind but the emotions. A feeling for good design is instinctive. But there are certain elements and principles of design which, when thought about and put into practice, will be helpful to those with lack of self-confidence. The elements of design important to the decoupeur are color, line, direction, shape, space, and value.

COLOR—See Chapter 3.

LINE— When you think of line, you think of a straight line, a curved line, a shaded line, a broken line, etc. In design, lines enclose the object to be decorated and enclose the shapes within your decoration.

SHAPE is determined by lines. The shape of the object you decoupage will determine the shapes used in your design. If your shapes are three-dimensional instead of two-dimensional, they are known as *mass*.

SPACE in decorative design is that portion of a design not covered by the decorative material. In decoupage, the bare spots between your cutouts constitute space.

VALUE is the relation of one part of a design to another with respect to lightness and darkness. In coloring your prints, for example, you were urged to follow the shadings put in by the artist. Thus, you are following the artist's own concept of value. In a design, value is not only part of color but is obtained by placement of light and dark shapes within your design. The elements of design must be so used as to create unity which may be obtained by dominance; by repetition and variety, or similarity and contrast; by proportion; by balance; by rhythm.

DOMINANCE is the life stream of a design; it expresses the purpose the artist has in mind. One shape in a design may dominate the others which are used to complement the dominant shape. Or one color may dominate. Or the shape of the object may be the dominant factor, with your decoration merely being used to emphasize or beautify this shape.

REPETITION or SIMILARITY are perhaps the easiest principles to put into effect in seeking unity. But too much repetition can become monotonous. This can be prevented by including VARIETY or CONTRAST in your design. Similar shapes, for example, can be varied by using different colors or shadings. Or a straight line of flowers forming a border can be varied by size and by curves within the border.

PROPORTION is the ratio of the size of one part of your design to another. It is the ratio of the size of one shape to another; or the ratio of shape to space. In decoupage, the proportion of your design is influenced by the proportions of the box or other item you intend to decorate.

BALANCE needs no definition. Everyone knows whether a design looks top-heavy or lopsided. Balance in a design is achieved or not achieved by the placement of the individual parts of your design. If, for example, you place a large cutout right of center and one the same size left of center, you have achieved balance through symmetry. But you may obtain just as good balance by placing the large cutout right of center and placing one or more smaller ones left of center.

RHYTHM comes from the Latin *"Rhythmus"* and the Greek *"Rhythmos,"* meaning flow. In a design it is achieved by the placement of one element in relation with another, by color selection, by accent. Again, it is something which we feel. It may be obtained obviously by repetition, or the entire design may have a flowing quality with a lovely, subtle rhythm.

A local decorator who teaches interior design throws up his hands in horror when one mentions the elements and principles of design. Each of his designs is good but he never consciously thinks of the elements and principles listed above. On the other hand, a friend of mine who has won all kinds of awards for her flower arrangements tells me that she never does an arrangement without thinking consciously of what she considers the five most important principles of flower design: *color, line, shape, proportion,* and *rhythm.*

Those who do decoupage know something of what goes into a good design, but must remember that designing and creating come from within. No piece of decoupage will become a personal piece of work until you have stopped copying and gone out on your own. Then only do you take the first step toward becoming creative. But the most important thing for a beginner to remember is that the design is good if it is effective for the purpose at hand. Look at the amusing box in Plate 10 with the physician urging the serpent to join its mate on the caduceus.

This is good design because it tells a story with simplicity and with humor. The box was chosen for a third-year medical student. The size and shape of the box itself are such that

Plate 10. Boxes done by Mrs. Louis How, Lakeville, Ind. The designs for the two boxes at the left are excellent examples of the personal touch in decoupage. The oblong box with half caduceus was done for a nephew in third-year medical school. The box with partridges was done for a friend whose hobby is wood carving. The sides are decorated with cutouts representing partially carved partridges and the top shows a finished carving.

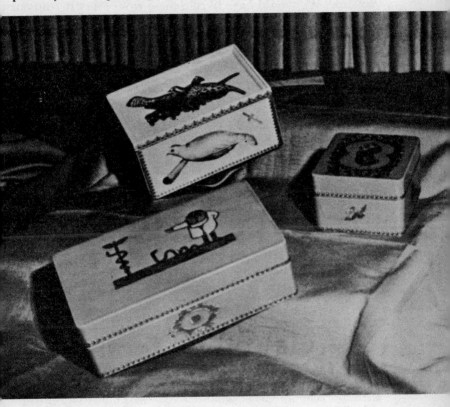

it can be used on a man's dresser or desk, and the design says "This is for a doctor-to-be."

Turn to the photographs in Part II of this book and examine each design critically. They were chosen from the many so generously submitted to illustrate variety in style, in objects suitable for decoupage, in material suitable for cutouts. They were also chosen from as many decoupeurs as possible. We should have liked a piece from every decoupeur in the country, but unfortunately, we know only a few of them and many of those we do know were too busy to have photographs taken. But our samples are widely diverse and you can teach yourself by selecting those you think excellent and studying them to find out why they appeal or why you instinctively selected them as good. When you find a design which you believe is poor, analyze that to see how it could be improved. Go through the photographs again and see the variety of uses made of the same print. There are several Pillement prints which have been used over and over but never in the same way. See also how the same tables or boxes look completely different when done in varying designs.

Get in the habit of thinking of design. Read books on design. Take instruction from a teacher known for good design. Work with friends whose taste you admire. Go to museums and look at good design. Don't be afraid to ask questions. Keep notes on what you see and learn. Start a file of pictures of good design which you have culled from magazines, newspapers, art books, photographs, etc. And practice designing on your own. Don't be ashamed to copy, but keep in mind that this is someone else's design and that you are copying in order to learn to strike out on your own.

Even when you have learned to design in a manner which satisfies you, you may not be creative. You may get a good design, for example, by simply taking prints of Pillement, who was a master of design, and transferring his design to a tray, table, or box. You have added nothing of yourself to the new design. You have simply recognized good design and used it for another purpose. But if you take a group of prints and cut them up and use cutouts in an entirely different way, you are beginning to create. Which plates at the back of the book show more than a knowledge of design? Decide for yourself and then discuss them with your friends or with your instructor.

In addition to knowing the elements of good design, it is helpful to the beginner to see some of the mechanics of a simple design. As an illustration, take a look at Plate 11, which shows a family letter box decorated with cutouts from copies of Jean Pillement's "Le Cinque Sens de Nature" (The Five Senses).

The prints were colored and cut out and laid on each panel to see how they would look. Plate 12 shows one print, after it was cut, laid on a piece of paper the exact size and shape of one of the five panels of the letter box.

You will see that the figure in the center is in good proportion for the panel. But the cartouche around the figure is not the right shape for the panel. This is simple to correct. Just cut up the border, as shown. Reassemble the pieces to form a curved line which follows the contour of the panel as shown in the lowest panel, Plate 11.

Now let's try a slightly more difficult job of selection and arrangement. A friend asked me to decorate a jewel box with birds. She chose the box shown in Plate 13 with top and one side up.

For decorating the box she selected the prints shown left and center in Plate 13.

Plate 11. Letter box by the author done with Pillement's "Five Senses" and used for teaching purposes.

Plate *12*.   *Copy of Pillement's "Le Gout" (Taste) shown whole
on the left; cut and laid on panel in center; and cut apart on
the right.*

Plate *13*.   *Unfinished boxes for decoupaging.*

Plate 14. Copy of bird print from Ladies' Amusement Book or The Whole Art of Japanning Made Easy, *published for Robert Sayer at the Golden Buck, London, 1760–62. The bird border is unsigned. The right-hand part of the photograph shows the border print cut up.*

Designing and Creating

After coloring and cutting two of the center, border print, and one of the bird print, I laid the cut-out bird print in the center section and laid one of the cut borders on the left panel. Plate 15 shows a piece of paper the size of the box with the two prints cut and laid on at left and center.

The beaded edging which surrounds the prints is of wood and is available at most lumber companies. Since I was asked to use this to frame the three panels, I had to place it on my paper pattern so that my spacing was right.

It is obvious from looking at the left panel that the bird border is much too heavy for the space. The next step was to

Plate 15. Bird print from Plate 14 cut and laid in center. Border print cut and laid on left panel. The right-hand panel shows the border redesigned from the cutouts on the right of Plate 14.

cut the print apart, and the right panel in Plate 14 shows what the print looked like when so cut. Now take a look at the right panel in Plate 15 and see how the new cutouts were used. This is still too heavy for the central theme, which is the birds upsetting the basket. Cut some more. Make the individual pieces slimmer. Plate 16 shows the result of this.

Notice the slim effect achieved in the designs on the side panels. Now look at the center and see what has been added to the bird print. The scroll of birds at the top and the conventional scroll design at the bottom were needed to fill some of the space around the birds. The poor little birds looked

Plate 16. Top of box in Plate 13 designed from prints in Plate 14 plus cutouts from a copy of a Watteau print.

lost before. The added cutouts came from a Watteau print. The bird scroll is good because it repeats the bird motif, but it would be much better had the birds been colored better. And the bottom scroll, which is good in line, is much too light in color. Further, the shadings have not been emphasized, as you were told to do in Chapter 3. Notice the difference between the lower middle scrolls and those on the sides. What else do you think is glaringly wrong with this design? Wouldn't it be greatly improved by the removal of the heavy border and the substitution of a more graceful one? And even if you do not remove this border, it should be the same color as the box so that it does not stand out so much.

In working for a design for the letter holder and the jewel box, we kept cutting for line, fit, etc. Take another look at the Plates 6 and 7 in Chapter 3. The borders in Plate 6 which were used on the tables in Plate 7 are two of the most versatile borders I have ever seen. On the tables, for example, you can find three different designs made from them—the border on the tops of the tables, the border on the sides of the tables, and the decoration on the legs. Plate 17 shows you two of the borders cut up to begin the design of the border on top.

The shapes are laid out on a paper the same size and shape as the table. Those below the arrow were the pieces selected to do the border on one side of the middle table. The actual border is shown below the selected shapes. The border for the sides of the table was made from similar pieces. But when it came to the legs, much smaller pieces were needed. It is obvious that, in cutting up any print to produce special pieces to fit into your design, you will end up with many

Plate 17. Cutouts from border prints shown in Plate 6 and laid on paper the size and shape of the middle table in Plate 7. The cutouts below the white line were the ones used to design the border shown on the table edge below the paper.

pieces not usable for that particular design. There are two lessons to be learned from this: 1) Save all bits and parts from every cut-out print; and 2) cut more prints than you think you will need. One of the most irritating things in decoupage is to get all ready to lay out a design and find you have to stop in the middle and color and cut more prints. On the tables, for example, I colored and cut up 40 border prints which, measured in length, gave me more than I thought I needed. But after cutting them up for my borders, I discovered that I didn't even have enough for two tables.

If you want to see other ways in which these same borders have been used, turn to Plates 35, 39, and 52 in Part II and you will find three other designs from them. Plate 35, for example, doesn't use it as a border at all but uses it to build up the sides of a panel. Here it looks like wrought iron.

Now let's look at a design which is an example of excellence. Turn to Plate 30 at the back of the book and examine this delightful panel which could have been designed and executed by the finest of 18th-century artists. The panel, you will note, was executed by Mrs. W. James Moore under the tutelage of Maybelle and Hiram Manning, two of the finest designers who have ever worked in decoupage. The picture as a whole has unity because it has balance, rhythm, proportion, similarity and variety. The central or dominating figure is the Roman horseman on his solid base which is tied in with the graceful side designs by a cartouche of flowers at the base. Only a designer sure of himself would have added the delicious, delicate umbrella and two angels to the Roman horseman. But what a whimsical touch and how perfect it is. Now look at the two side designs with their upward sweep. Examine these in detail and see how too much repetition has been avoided by the placement of individual shapes and by use of a variety of shapes. Think of *space* and see how the artists have filled part of the space above the horseman's head with a spray of flowers falling from the top drape. Finally, in proportion and rhythm, the design is perfection.

For another type of excellent design, look at those of Alice Balterman (See Part II). Here is an artist who achieves a feeling of the modern through use of old prints, cards, theatre programs, etc. Some are exceptionally good examples of the trompe l'oeil (fooling the eye) technique. All are examples of creative art.

In the work illustrations given, you will note that I have set up the designs on a separate piece of paper the same size and shape as the object to be decorated. In practice, however, I design directly on the object because it saves time. You may select either method. If you choose to design on paper, measure where the central or large pieces are from your border and put a guide mark on the object itself. Chalk is good because it can be rubbed off easily if you get the mark in the wrong place. Even when you are designing directly on your object, it is well to measure. This is particularly true where you are designing with two identical or similar portions of a design. Just don't trust your eye. It's so easy to measure.

If you design directly on your object, fasten the cutouts with base tape or a similar product. Base tape is waxed on both sides, adheres with pressure, and can be easily removed without hurting paper, wood, metal, glass, etc. You will find it invaluable in laying on a design.

When you have your design worked out completely, lift up one piece at a time, take off the tape, brush glue all over the underside of the piece, and put it back down, using pressure from the center toward the edges so that it will be glued down evenly and all excess glue will be squeezed out. By having the entire design before you, it is easy to fit each piece into place because the rest of the design gives you your guideposts.

For glue I prefer a water-soluble white glue with a resin base. But you may use any type which works for you. My choice is Duratite, which is manufactured by Dap, Inc. When you use this, it is easy to clean up excess glue. This may be done with a sponge dipped in warm water or, if the glue has hardened for some time, try vinegar. If I am designing with small pieces, such as the border in Plate 17, I find it easier to apply the glue with a small brush directly to each cutout. If you permit the glue to get slightly tacky before putting on each piece, you will find you get less glue oozing out around the edges of the pieces as you put them on. It is most important to see that every piece is glued down tight because otherwise you will either get bubbles or your edges will curl.

As you put on each piece, start in the middle and exert pressure from the center to each edge. Some glue will be forced out. You may use your fingers, your fingernails, or a small instrument. I use my fingers and fingernails because I think I can feel whether the piece is really tight. But any wooden tool with a wedge-shaped end is good. One of my friends uses a nickel whose edges have become rounded with age. The only caution in using tools is not to use them with such force that they scratch the print or the object you are working on.

When it comes to putting on large pieces, the problem is more difficult. There are two ways of handling such pieces.

You may smear glue over the entire surface of the object where you plan to place your cutout or you may put glue on part of the print and gradually glue the entire piece. The former method is much faster insofar as the actual gluing is concerned. But the latter method will save time when it comes to cleaning up after the piece has been glued fast.

If you use the former method, add some glycerine to your glue before you smear the glue on the surface of the object to be decorated. The purpose of this is to slow down the drying time of the glue and to make it slippery so that you can slide your print around and get it exactly where you want it. I use about one part glycerine to four parts glue. When you have the print centered, begin at the middle of the print and press down from center to outside of each portion of the print.

When you are sure the print is secure, look it over to see that you have left no air bubbles. If you find these, slit the piece with a sharp knife and insert glue on a toothpick in the cut and reglue, pressing hard so that the cut edges meet and leave no sign of having been cut. This takes care, but is not difficult. One of my students came up with an ingenious method of dealing with bubbles. She covered a large chest with tortoiseshell paper and left it to dry. Next day she was horrified to find bubbles decorating one entire side of the chest. Nothing daunted, she marched herself to a nearby drugstore, procured a hypodermic needle, and set to work. She used the needle to prick each bubble and draw out the air before inserting glue. It work beautifully. Of course, her husband was a little shaken to come home and find her jabbing at the chest with a hypodermic needle but most husbands have learned to accept the fantastic when their wives do decoupage. Sometimes you overlook a spot where a fine stem is puckered up. The only think you can do with this is to cut the pucker through in the middle and then cut off enough from each piece to let the two pieces meet in the middle when pressed down.

The next step is to begin to clean off the excess glue with a sponge dipped in warm water or vinegar. Cleaning around the outside edges is simple but getting the glue cleaned off in between each part of the design is tedious. A good method to try is to dip a Q-tip into vinegar and work carefully in between each part until all the glue is off. After cleaning, be sure to check your entire print again to be sure you have not loosened any part of it while cleaning.

If you select the second method of gluing—that is, putting the glue on the cutout, you will be wise to have a helper when gluing a large piece. Turn again to Plate 7 and look at the center piece on top. This was put on in one piece. By far the easiest way would be to smear glue on the table in the rectangle where you intend to place the cutout. But if you plan to glue the paper, begin at the top, the bottom, or either side, and put glue on a portion, going all the way across the side you choose and smearing glue on for about one inch. Place this on the table, which must have been marked with chalk, and glue down tight. The helper, meanwhile, holds the design up while you are working. When you have finished, the helper puts glue on another small section and you again smooth it down tight. This process is continued until the entire design is finished. I personally would never use this method except on small pieces, but many of my students prefer it and there is no question but that the clean-up time at the end is cut drastically.

Now, what if you finish gluing on a design and find that it is not in line? Or what if you decide it is not appropriate? In the first case, you may possibly correct it by adding bits and pieces to bring it into alignment. One of my students, for instance, put on a grape border which was much farther from the edge of the box at the top left-hand side than it was from the lower left-hand side. We corrected this by adding a few tendrils, bringing them toward the edge of the box. But if the design is large and really on crooked, all you can do is to soak it off with warm water. A sponge dipped in warm water is excellent for this purpose. And there is nothing you can do about a design which is improper but to soak it off. If you work carefully, you may save your entire design. I find, however, that this takes so much time and is so nerve-wracking that I prefer to just get it off and throw it away. But I love to color and cut so I am never disturbed if I have to redo something. Most persons disagree with me and are willing to take the time and care needed to save a design which has been glued on. After you get it off, turn it upside down and let it dry.

The Finishing Touches

Painted borders, gold-leaf borders, colored lines, mother-of-pearl, and other trim and ornament were employed in the 18th century to enhance the beauty of a design done with cutouts. Today we can use all these plus many new products developed in the 20th century for decorative purposes.

The Venetian secretary in the Frontispiece, you will note, was done with painted scrolls, gold leaf, and cutouts. The scrolls and the gold-leaf trim are an integral part of the design. In all good design, nothing is added which does not "belong." Your trim, no matter what it is, must be more than just an added thought. It must be right for the rest of your design.

If you want to paint a scroll such as that used in the Frontispiece, draw in your double lines and paint, as instructed in Chapter 3. You will also find how to gold-leaf in that chapter. A far easier method of getting a gold-leaf effect is to use Treasure Gold, which can be put on with your fingers and buffed with a soft cloth fifteen minutes after it has been applied.

If you want to outline a box or design with a gold line or a line in any other color, one way to do it is to use a ruler turned on its edge as a guide. Dip a thin quill brush about 1½" long into the color you are using and brush it along the ruler, pulling the brush toward you. A far easier way to get a line in any color you wish is use your color pencils. Not only can you use the pencils for a fine line of a contrasting or accent color but you can use them for wide borders. The tray in Plate 61, for example, has a border inside the gold-paper braid which edges the tray. The inside border is a deep blue and was colored with pencil. Be sure, when you use pencils, that your area is covered completely with color and that no pencil marks show. For such work, use a pencil which is dull with a rounded point.

Gold-paper trims, manufactured in West Germany and available in decoupage studios, craft supply houses, and many gift shops, come in widths varying from several inches to a narrow fine line. Although these come in a bright gold, they may be painted any color you wish. Even when you want a gold line, it is well to dull or soften the original gold. The softest gold spray I have found is that put out by the Illinois Bronze Company.

You may prefer an antique look. This can be obtained by wiping the braid with white, raw umber, burnt umber, Venetian red, or a blue-green. What you use depends on your original colors and the background color of the object you are decorating.

When gluing on gold-paper trims, put guidelines on the object where they are to go and put glue on the back of a strip of gold-paper braid. Let the glue set for a few minutes until it becomes tacky and then apply the strip to your object, using pressure to get it glued down tight. A word of warning, however. Thin your glue with a little water before applying. The braid is thick and the less glue you have under it the smoother you can get it down. Unless these trims are glued down tight and smoothed with a small roller or something similar, you will find that your varnish is likely to puddle around them. This is to be avoided no matter how long it takes you to get your braid on so that it is smooth and tight.

The great advantage of using gold-paper trims is that they come in such a variety of designs, such as Greek key, rope, chain, etc. Some of these were copied from old designs and others are modern. A substitute for the straight-edged braids which are used in place of painted lines may be made from paper the same thickness as your prints. Take a sheet of paper and, with a yardstick, rule lines the width of the trim you want. Suppose you want a ⅛" edging. Draw lines down the length of the paper ⅛" apart. Draw the lines with India ink so that they are very dark. Now paint with a brush, spray paint, or color with pencils the entire sheet on the opposite side from which you have drawn the lines. Cut along your lines and you have excellent decorative strips.

Other materials for decorative borders include metal strips, plastic strips, and wood strips. If you plan to use any of these, do not glue them on until your piece is varnished since such raised borders make your varnishing much more difficult. If you use a metal strip, for example, paint it the color you want. Varnish it separately and rub it down (3 coats of varnish are usually sufficient). When your varnishing is finished on the box or other object, sand down the edge where the strip is to go and glue it on. Look for metal strips, plastic strips, and wood strips in hardware stores, lumber yards, craft shops, and decoupage studios.

Mother-of-pearl can be most effective with a decoupage design. Plate 34, for example, shows a miniature chest with mother-of-pearl used at the long corners. Mother-of-pearl leaves which were used for this come from the inside lining of certain mollusks and are available at some craft shops and at decoupage studios. They are brittle and must be softened either in boiling water or vinegar before they can be cut to size.

Assume that you want to cover a corner of an octagonal box with mother-of-pearl. The corner measures 1" by 2". Cut a piece of paper to this size. Have boiling water ready and take up a mother-of-pearl leaf with tweezers or small tongs. Dip it into the boiling water and let it stay about a minute. Take it out and lay your paper pattern on it and cut the mother-of-pearl according to your pattern. If you are cutting a larger piece, the mother-of-pearl leaf may become brittle before you have finished. Put it back into the boiling water and soften it again.

If you use vinegar, the mother-of-pearl will stay soft for a long time. You may find, however, that the vinegar has taken away some of the iridescence. This may be restored by spraying with Barrier.

When it comes to gluing on a piece of mother-of-pearl, you will find that each piece curves slightly. Glue with the curve toward the object and flatten with your fingers as you glue.

Mother-of-pearl may also be used for inlaid borders. For such borders, it will be necessary to cut many small pieces and fit them together. This will be easier if you will cut paper patterns for your pieces, fit them into your border and then cut your mother-of-pearl. Leave the paper patterns, which you have numbered, on each piece of mother-of-pearl until you are ready to glue the whole design in.

6

How to Varnish

THE FINAL PROCESSES OF DECOUPAGE—varnishing and rubbing down—are the most tedious steps of all. But the care with which we varnish or lacquer and the amount of elbow grease we put into sanding and steel-wooling will mean the difference between a half-baked-looking piece of decoupage and a professional-looking one. Indeed, I have seen decoupage done by an amateur who colored with indifference and cut abominably but who ended up with good-looking pieces because her designs were good and her finishes superb.

The finishes used today are equal or superior to those of 18th-century Europe but they are completely different from the vegetable lacquers of the Orient. What 18th-century European artisans sought was a lacquer which would compare favorably with those of China and Japan. The lacquers from these countries came from the same source—the sap of a tree called "rhus vernicifers." The tree, while indigenous to China, was transplanted into Japan. Japanese lacquers were superior in quality to those of China, probably because the Japanese refined the sap better. But the lacquer ware, or decorated lacquers, of Japan were not equal to those of China except where the Japanese worked with gold. The Chinese used more colors and their decorative work as a whole surpassed in quality that of the Japanese. The choice of the English word for the lacquers which were invented to copy Oriental lacquers was "japanning" because of the superiority of the lacquer itself, not of the decorative lacquer ware.

The Encyclopaedia Britannica, under the word "lacquer," states specifically that the article which follows deals with "artistic lacquer ware"—that is, the decorative lacquer objects so widely sought after in Europe in the 17th and 18th centuries. The reader is referred to "varnish" to find a discussion of our modern lacquers which, according to the encyclopaedia, are transparent finishes for wood. Under "varnish" are also included shellac and plastic coatings. In other words, all the finishes which we use today in decoupage are included under varnish. We shall use the term varnish, however, to refer only to varnishes which are so labeled by the manufacturer and shall differentiate between varnish, lacquer, and plastic coating. The important point here is that our modern covers are entirely different from the lacquers of the 18th century.

The lacquers used by the Orientals could be built up and hardened to such an extent that they could be carved, as witness the magnificient Coromandel, or Bantam, screens. The names for the screens and other carved Chinese work came into existence because they were imported from Bantam on the coast of Coromandel. In this work, color was laid under the layers of lacquer and when the lacquer was sufficiently built up, carvings were made deep enough to go down to the original color. The different colors were put in on several different layers of lacquer so that one color could appear higher or deeper than another. The artist had to know exactly where to carve. There could be no mistakes.

In *Lacquer, Oriental and Western, Ancient and Western*, published by The Cooper Union Museum for the Arts of Decoration, 1951, it is explained that our modern varnishes and lacquers are nothing more than "films of pigment" which emphasize the planes to which they are applied. On the other hand, the vegetable lacquers used by the Chinese, Japanese and other Orientals was "a means of investing a surface with profound depths, unaided by perspective or illusion."

Despite the fact that Europeans never produced a lacquer (and what they produced is more like our modern varnish than our modern lacquer) to equal that of the Chinese, they nevertheless came up with some fine products, of which the best was the "vernis Martin," a varnish which bears the name of the five Martin brothers who invented and manufactured it. The term "vernis Martin" is used in France today to refer to 18th-century lacquers and lacquer ware. Other fine lacquers—or varnishes—were produced in Holland, England, Belgium, Germany and Italy. When the decorated Oriental lacquers were first copied in Europe, all types of decoration were attempted. But it was the painted lacquer ware which became most popular and it was this lacquer ware which the Italians began to imitate with "lacche povero"—which we now call decoupage.

The depth which is naturally acquired by use of the vegetable lacquers of the Far East can be simulated by decoupeurs today. In fact, I believe that much of the modern decoupage has a better finish than that of the decoupage of the 18th century. Although the application of coat after coat of varnish over a plain surface will not bring continued depth, the same application over cutouts does give us the illusion of depth, and much of our present-day work in flat surfaces has a feeling of three-dimension because of this. Unrestored, early decoupage which I have seen does not have the finish which you find on good decoupage today. There are three ways to finish a piece of decoupage: 1) varnish; 2) lacquer; and 3) plastic coatings, for what I call "quickies." The latter is not for permanent work but for such things as handbags, Christmas tree ornaments, etc.

VARNISHING

Having checked for a final time to see if all your cutouts are glued down tight with no bubbles and with all edges completely flat, cover the design with a solution of one part shellac and one part alcohol and let dry for at least 12 hours. Rub down with 0000 steel wool and clean the surface well with a lintless cloth. You are now ready to varnish. When selecting varnishes for covering a piece of decoupage, get only the finest quality and get a varnish which is not fast drying. Although I use a flat varnish, you may use a glossy or semi-glossy one and still end up with a soft-dull finish provided you use fine enough steel wool and are willing to put in extra hours of rubbing down. I find the flat varnishes require less rubbing down.

The reason for avoiding a varnish which dries too quickly is that these varnishes are not as durable as the slower-drying ones. One other word about buying varnish. Buy it in as small a quantity as possible since, once a can is opened, the varnish deteriorates. Open up a can of your choice and thin it with mineral spirits. This is a tip I got from George Grotz in his book *The Furniture Doctor*. It has been an invaluable one. I use two tablespoons of mineral spirits to one-half pint varnish. And before closing a can of varnish, I skim the top of it with mineral spirits.

Using a small brush (½″ for small objects to 2″ for large pieces), dip your brush into the varnish and let it get completely covered. Now flow the varnish onto the surface, letting each stroke go in the same direction. Work on a flat surface wherever possible. Check for hairs which may have come from your brush and pick them up, using your brush flat, or almost horizontal. Check for runs and brush them out before the varnish begins to harden. Let dry for at least 24 hours, no matter what the directions on the can of varnish tell you. Work in a room close to 70 degrees. In Florida, where the humidity is frequently high, I always work in either a heated or air-conditioned room.

Now that's the most frequently advocated way of varnishing. But George Grotz found another way from a man whom he described as "being a lad of about eighty-two years." He watched the man varnishing transoms on a boat and saw him brushing the varnish in as hard as he could and even working up a lather with his varnish. Mr. Grotz writes: "Naturally, I asked him some questions, and got him to talk about the performance I had just witnessed. 'The secret is,' he said, 'that you always thin varnish with a couple of dollops of thinner.' (This turned out to be about one part mineral spirits to seven or eight parts of varnish.) 'Then,' he went on, 'you have to really scrub it in, because this stiffens the varnish so it won't sag. And the bubbles disappear because you thin the varnish.' "*

I found this hard to believe, but I tried it. It works. Mr. Grotz tells the reader to brush hard in one direction and then "tip" off the varnish by going in the other direction with the brush held almost vertical so that just the tip of the brush is used. Try it. It's one of the easiest methods of varnishing I know. But one word of caution: This method will require more coats than the first method I described. So it's up to you.

After each coat of varnish is applied, let it dry 24 hours. Put on at least 10 coats before you begin to sand or to smooth with steel wool. But do not begin to sand—even after 10 coats—if your design is not completely sunk into the varnish so that you cannot feel it. If you have used thick prints, you may need 15 or more coats of varnish before sanding. One of the best finishes I ever obtained was not sanded until 20 coats of varnish had been applied. But I find this risky and I also find that the total amount of sanding will be less if you do some sanding after each coat of varnish beyond the 10th.

Sand first with wet or dry Tri-m-ite No. 400 or with Carborundum No. 400, using either of these soaking wet. You may use a coarser grained sandpaper for your first sanding if you prefer, but I use nothing coarser than No. 400. Your sanding will be smoother if you will wrap small pieces of sandpaper around a small block of wood and use this in rubbing down. There are also commercial hand sanders on the market which are made to hold your sandpaper flat and smooth. When you have sanded the surface smooth, wash it off, let it dry, and wipe it clean. Rub down with 0000 steel wool, using it dry, until there are no imperfections and the

*George Grotz, *The Furniture Doctor*. New York: E. P. Dutton, 1962.

surface has a soft, dull glow. Use small pieces of steel wool and rub down with a circular motion. When the surface is glass smooth, wipe it off, and when it is free of all dirt and completely dry, you are ready for more varnishing. Continue varnishing and sanding down until the entire surface, including the cutouts, is flat. When you can no longer feel any edges on the cutouts, you are ready for the final sanding, steel-wooling, and waxing.

Use any good paste wax. Put the wax on with a damp (not wet) cloth. Use as little wax as possible and rub one small area with a circular motion until you get the sheen you desire.

If you want a high polish, you can obtain it by omitting the waxing and using steel wool dipped in a commercial finishing compound. Sherwin-Williams, Wilson Imperial, and DuPont have excellent compounds. Buy only white ones. By wetting steel wool and dipping it into these compounds, you get an abrasive action. But if you use the steel wool dry and dip it into the compound, you can obtain a high polish on your object. This gives an excellent finish for trays but often produces too high a polish for furniture. No waxing is needed when this method is used.

Some decoupeurs use spray varnishes with good effects. If you want to try any of the spray varnishes, remember that you will have to put on many more coats before beginning to sand, because each coat is much thinner than that of brushing varnish. However, you may apply several coats each day. All spray cans, whether paint, lacquer, plastic, or varnish, should be used in an upright position and held about a foot away from the object you intend to spray. Be sure that the object is also upright. If, for example, you are spraying a table top, turn the table so that the top is at right angles to your spray can. Spray cans have complete directions for using. Read them.

LACQUER

Lacquer has one advantage over varnish—it dries much more quickly. But lacquer cannot be applied over many paints, over shellac, or over varnish. One of the top decoupeurs of our day, Lucy Herndon Crockett, used it exclusively in her decoupage. Unfortunately, examples of Miss Crockett's work are unavailable because she did not keep any samples when she gave up decoupage. In a delightful little pamphlet entitled "Decoupage, the Pleasures and Perplexities of Decorating with Paper Motifs," Miss Crockett explained that not only did she find lacquer the best finish but that she used it as an adhesive. Because lacquer over most painted surfaces will make them bubble or crackle, Miss Crockett usually used flat black paint as a background and prepared this before she brushed on her first coat of lacquer by spraying with several thin coats of lacquer so that the surface was "set." When these were dry, a coat of clear, thick brushing lacquer was applied and the cutouts were placed directly onto this lacquered surface and moved about with a sharp instrument until they were in place. This method is not for a beginner, however. More coats of lacquer were applied after the design was in place and dry. For the final coats, Miss Crockett added a flatting agent to the lacquer so that her finish was not shiny but as soft as that we get with varnish. In fact, Miss Crockett says that she preferred lacquer to varnish because she could get a hand-rubbed look which she was unable to get with varnish. Lacquer will not give you as hard and as durable a finish as varnish and it is much more likely to deteriorate because of changes in weather.

A new lacquer finish called "King's Decoupage Finish" has been on the market for little less than a year. This finish is by far the best lacquer finish I have found. It goes on very smoothly and it is possible to apply four or more coats a day. I recommend this highly to decoupeurs who want to have their colors remain practically unchanged after the finishing process is completed. There is also a sealer which should be used before applying the lacquer. It is advisable, however, to use a lacquer base paint when using any lacquer finish.

PLASTIC COATINGS

I have a mental picture of a reader reaching this point and throwing up his hands in horror at the very idea of covering a gorgeous design with plastic. Plastic is not for fine furniture, trays, etc., but it is excellent for those projects which are made only for temporary use, such as Christmas tree balls, handbags, etc. And I have used it to seal a design under glass-top tables which I knew would be used outdoors near salt water. The plastic spray I use is called "Blair" and is manufactured by Blair Art Products, Inc., Memphis, Tenn. It is waterproof when dry and is used as a protective coating on all types of boats, on tools, and even on buildings. The Christmas tree ball in Plate 26 was sprayed inside and out with Barrier, which prevents tranishing and may be sprayed over velvet, rhinestones, glitter, gold-and-silver braids as well as over paper. It dries to the touch within 20 minutes, but it will not become fully hardened for 48 hours. If you use it, therefore, spray on as many coats as you wish in a day. But do not touch the finished product for 48 hours. As with any other spray, always spray with the can upright and with the object at right angles to the spray.

AVOIDING AND CORRECTING MISTAKES

Whether you are using varnish, lacquer, or plastic for a covering for your cutouts, always work in a good light with the object being worked on between you and the light or with the light overhead. The first box I ever varnished was done in a cellar where the heater gave me a good warm working place but where the light was very poor. I varnished every day for fifteen days and thought I was doing a fine job. But when I took the box up to the living room to show my husband, I was horrified to find that it was literally covered with runs. In fact, there were so many runs that it looked as though they were the design and a most unattractive design they made. Had I been working in a good light this would never have happened. They could have been brushed out before the varnish set or could have been lightly sanded out had I caught them after the varnish had set but before I applied another coat. Rather than try to get rid of all these runs on my little box, I simply continued varnishing and sanded like mad at the end. The runs never completely disappeared and the box is kept as a horrible example for my students.

The moral is not only to varnish with care and in a good light but always to check before applying the next coat. If, for example, you find a run in a coat of varnish applied that day, you can sand lightly and then go over the spot with mineral spirits. This will take out the run.

If, by chance, you drop a piece of decoupage just after you have finished varnishing it, the easiest way to repair the damage is to wipe off the entire object with mineral spirits immediately. Then start over with your varnishing.

If you are lacquering, a mistake in lacquer must be corrected with lacquer thinner. Lacquer thinner is also the solvent for Blair.

7

Working On and Under Glass

Flat Work, Elevations, and Shadowboxes

Of all the projects in decoupage, the one which can be done most expeditiously is a simple design under glass with a painted background behind the design. One coat of varnish to seal the paint completes the project. But decoupage in which glass is used also includes shadow boxes where three-dimensional effects are achieved by stuffing and molding your cutouts or by employing elevations.

Let's try a flat piece first. A service plate is easy. Have a piece of glass 1/4″ thick cut in a circle 12″ or 14″ in diameter. Color and cut three roses for the center, and color and cut enough small flowers to make a circular border for the outside of the plate. Lay your design on a circle of wax paper cut exactly the size of the glass. Smear glue on one side of your glass after the glass has been thoroughly cleaned and place the glued side over the wax-paper circle which contains your design. The glue will pick up the design but won't stick to the wax paper. Hold the glass up so that you can see the design through the glass. If the design has slipped, turn the glass over and move the individual pieces back into place. When the design is where you want it, lay the glass face down with the cutouts facing you and press down each one as instructed in the section on gluing in Chapter 5. Let the glass and the cutouts dry and wash off the excess glue with warm water or vinegar. Test every piece of the design with your fingers to be sure each is glued down fast. Any unglued edges will permit paint to run under and obscure the cutouts. When you are sure your design is on tight and your glass is clean, you are ready to put on a coat of protective before painting. Use one part shellac and one part denatured alcohol as a protective or use a good commercial protective. There are many new ones on the market and you should ask your decoupage studio, your paint store, or your art supply house to recommend the best.

In painting on a background for a small piece such as our plate, hold the plate on edge with the design facing a mirror and apply your paint. For larger pieces it is better to raise the object sufficiently to get your hand under for painting. This leaves the design facing you so that you can see that you are getting the paint on smoothly. When the paint is dry, check to see whether you need a second coat, which is sometimes necessary to hide brush marks or spots you have missed the first time. Apply the second coat, if needed, let it dry, and then put on a coat of varnish to seal it. Let this dry 24 hours and your project is finished.

The three-tiered glass jar in Plate 18 was done by putting the cutouts inside each glass section and painting in a white background. Where you are working on a curved surface,

*Plate 18. Three-tiered jar decorated by Mrs. Irving Swigart,
Sarasota, Fla. Pillement and other 18th-century prints were colored in soft pastels. The background is white.*

such as this, you have to exert even more care to get your prints glued down evenly and smoothly. Sometimes it is necessary to cut apart some pieces to accomplish this. Don't hesitate to cut since, when the design is glued back in, the cut will not show.

There is no problem about painting in your background for a project such as this since the design will always be facing you and you simply paint in back of it, being sure that your paint covers evenly. Don't brush too much. Pat the paint on by holding the end of the handle and letting the brush "pat" against the glass. If you see any runs between the cutouts and the glass, stop and clean off the paint around this section with a sponge or rag dipped in mineral spirits. When you have a space cleaned off so that you won't become covered with paint, lift up the piece of cutout which has paint on it and wipe off with mineral spirits. Now reglue, let dry, and continue with your paint job. Sometimes you will not discover a run until the whole job has been done and your paint is dry. The only thing to do in such cases is to scrape off the paint with a sharp knife or to soak the area in mineral spirits until the paint begins to soften. In such cases, you may not be able to lift the print without tearing it. The best thing to do is to take off an entire section and recolor and recut a piece to fit in. For example, in Plate 18, suppose that you found the head of the bird in the center of the top tier covered with paint. It might be easier to remove the paint around the entire bird and take off the whole bird and replace him with another since the pieces of this design are so small.

Usually a solid color or gold or silver leaf (see Chapter 3) are chosen for background. But some of the most arresting effects in decoupage are achieved by a multicolor back-

Plate 19. *Mirror done by Dorothy Harrower, Upper Black Eddy, Pa., for the author. This is an excellent example of decoupage under glass. The mirror was an old one with glass panels on either side. Mrs. Harrower used cutouts from Roman empress prints and painted in back of the cutouts to obtain the stunning cloud effects. Paints used included blue-greens, umbers, whites, and gold. Mrs. Harrower is a master of this technique.*

ground such as the cloud effect in Plate 19. This effect was achieved by use of ultramarine blue, green, raw umber, burnt sienna, white, and gold. Mrs. Harrower, who did the mirror panels for me, used colors which would pick up and highlight the colors in my living room. In working for this cloud effect, I have tried many methods. The following is the easiest I have found but it will take practice to achieve what you want.

Let us suppose that you are doing a set of glass-top tables and have decorated them with cutouts of Roman horsemen for a man's den. The den has browns with deep red accents which are on the henna side but very deep. Choose for your background colors Venetian red, burnt umber, yellow ochre, white, and gold. Squeeze a little of each color into small containers, using one container for a color. Now start with a one-inch brush and dip it into a small amount of varnish and pick up some of the deepest color, or raw umber. Dip it next into Venetian red, and put the Venetian red beside the raw umber. Continue, using the same brush until you have a bit of each color, except gold, on. Now swirl your brush over all these colors, using more varnish if needed to make the paints spread more easily. When you get a cloud effect you like, leave it alone. Take a clean brush and dip it into gold and outline the cloud. Continue until you have covered the glass. If you find an area too light or too dark, simply dip the brush into a dark or light paint and work the color you need into the light or dark area.

By swirling your brush around, you can get amazingly lovely effects. Dip your brush into varnish occasionally so that your paint slips around more easily. It will take lots of practice to get effects as good as those in the mirror in Plate 19. Dorothy Harrower is an expert in this technique. But,

Working On and Under Glass

although you may never approach her perfection, you can get good effects with practice. This cloud-type painting under glass is very effective in tables and lamps.

Lamps are not difficult to do but the unitiated are frequently completely baffled by them, asking again and again how you got the prints into them. Start with a hurricane globe, either a curved one, such as that in Plate No. 20 or a

Plate 20. Lamp by Mrs. Richard Clark, Louisville, Ky. The background is turquoise. The Pillement print is uncolored and the Chippendale borders are done with Treasure Gold.

Plate 21. Lamp by the author. The central figures are from a copy of a Piranesi Greek frieze. The borders are the same ones used in Plate 7. Both the figures and the central figures are gold (see Chapter 3, p. 66) and the background is off-white.

straight one such as that in Plate No. 21. Or you may use a shape, such as that shown in Plate 22, which is closed at one end. In choosing bases for lamps which you intend to decorate on the inside, be sure that the opening or openings are large enough for your hands to get into easily.

Let's assume that we are doing a lamp open at both ends. When you have colored and cut your prints, place design on the outside of the lamp, using base tape to hold the design on. When it is set up to your liking, and you are ready to put it inside the glass, smear a large area with glue to which you

Plate 22.   Glass, plain and decorated, for lamp by Patricia E. Nimocks, Louisville, Ky. Unfinished.

have added glycerin. Now lift part of the design off the outside of the glass and put it into the inside face up. Plate No. 23 looks ridiculous, but it is included so that you can see how messy the process is. You have to get in all over. The rose, as you can see, is clear in one part but cloudy in another. The white glue you use will dry clear but the clear part of the rose is where I have pressed out the excess glue and the cloudy part is where the glue has yet to be pressed out. Start in the center of your cutout and put pressure on with your fingers (which must be kept clean so as not to get

Plate 23. The author's hands thrust into a hurricane lamp, the inside of which is smeared with glue. The purpose of this photograph is to convince the reader that no matter how messy it looks, eventually all comes out in the wash. See text.

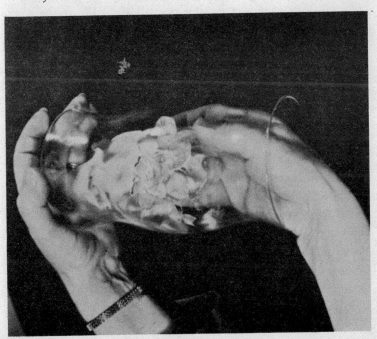

stuck to the print), smoothing the cutout from center to edges. As you get the excess glue out, the cutout becomes clear and you can tell whether you have all the excess out by the clarity of the print.

Bill Stewart, the photographer who did all the Sarasota pictures, suggested Plate 23 after I told him the story of a customer—not a student—who called me up and said the glue I sold her couldn't be right because she couldn't see her cutouts through it. As a matter of fact, the glue is particularly good for working under glass because it is opaque when wet and dries clear. If you cannot see your print under glass because of the glue between you and the print, you have not pressed down hard enough on your print to get excess glue out.

When the print is glued on, let it dry completely. Now comes the process of cleaning out all the glue in between your cutouts. Use a small piece of sponge dipped in warm vinegar. For tiny areas, use a Q-tip dipped in warm vinegar. If you are painting the background with a cloud effect, as described, you do not have to bother with much cleaning up of glue since it will not show. But if you are using a plain background, it is important that all glue be removed before you begin painting. When all glue is off, check the prints to be sure they are still glued tightly. A bubble in the middle of one, for example, is just as bad as not having the edges down tight. Why the paint will get into a bubble in the center of a print is a mystery to me but it will do it. Let dry thoroughly—but don't put it in the oven as one of my students did, with the result that she scorched the entire design.

Before putting on the background paint, coat each print with varnish or a plastic coating, being careful not to let the coating run over the edges but letting it come just to the edge of each print. This will prevent many paint runs underneath your cutouts. Again dry thoroughly.

When you are ready to paint, cover a table with newspapers and place the glass cylinder on the covered table with an open end facing you. Use a 1″ paint brush about 8″ to 10″ long. In painting in the background for lamps, I prefer my paint thicker than usual. Where I usually thin my paints with mineral spirits before brushing it on a wood surface, I leave it as thick as it comes when painting the inside of a lamp. Frequently you can do the job with only one coat of paint. Get your brush full of paint and, beginning halfway up the inside of the lamp (about where the lower hand is in Plate 23), pat on the paint with the brush. Work on the surface facing toward you. As you cover one area from halfway up to the bottom, roll the cylinder and continue covering from the center to the bottom. When you have covered all around the cylinder, turn it the other way round and do the second half just as you did the first half.

If you find you are getting streaks from brush marks, you are brushing the paint on rather than patting it on. The patting motion will come after practice. But don't worry if you have brush marks, since a second coat of paint under the first will correct this.

Sometimes—in fact, all too frequently—paint will run under your design. If this happens, stop painting immediately, wipe off as much paint as you can around the area where the run has occurred, and clean off an area around it with mineral spirits. Now carefully lift that part of the cutout where the paint ran under and obscured your design. Put mineral spirits on a Q-tip and clean off the paint on your design. Reglue the design. Do not continue painting until the reglued section is completely dry. It will not hurt your paint job to let part of the paint dry before you continue. If, however, you find that there seems to be a ridge where the first part of the paint job joins the second part, soften the ridge with mineral spirits and brush out the ridge. Then continue as directed.

In addition to working under glass, you can put your decoupage cutouts on top of glass. This is sometimes done to decorate mirror corners, for example. Seal your cutouts before putting them on either with varnish or with a plastic spray.

The most effective work in decoupage on top of glass, however, is that in which gesso has been applied to the outside of the glass first. (See Chapter 2 on applying gesso.) If cutouts are put on a gessoed piece of glass and then varnished, the effect is very much like porcelain. I prefer to tint my gesso the desired color before applying it, but it can be put on in its natural white color and painted over.

There are two ways of getting three-dimensional effects in shadow boxes. One is by elevations, which give a feeling of depth and space. This is called, for no reason I can find except that the term was used in 18th- and 19th-century Europe, *"Vue d'optique"* (literally—a view of the eye). In the early days, much of this technique was done without the use of cutouts, but the word has been adopted by decoupeurs to refer to our three-dimensional pictures featuring elevations.

The second method of getting a three-dimensional effect is by stuffing and molding figures, flowers, birds, etc., so that they become three-dimensional themselves. This method is sometimes combined with the first.

Vue d'Optique or Elevations

The gay little shadow box in Plate 24 was made from cut-

Plate 24. Three-dimensional picture done by author from cutouts from Joan Walsh Anglund's Spring Is a New Beginning. *See text.*

outs from *Spring Is a New Beginning.** Plate 25 shows the box with only the background glued in. The various cutouts used to make our three-dimensional picture are on the table, together with instruments and materials necessary to finish. Between the little girl and the little boy (Plate 25) is what looks like a glob of nothing. This is the white rabbit to whom

* Copyright ⓒ by Joan Walsh Anglund, 1963. Used with the permission of Harcourt, Brace and World, Inc., New York.

Plate 25. *Background and other cutouts to be used for three-dimensional picture in Plate 24. See text.*

the little girl is pointing in the final picture (Plate 24). The "glob" was made from three layers of cork glued together and glued to the back of the rabbit. If we put the picture together step by step, you will see how easy the process is.

First determine where each figure and cutout is to go. Now cut out pieces of cork, which can be obtained from craft supply stores, and glue them to the back of your figures. Use a greater thickness of cork for those figures which are to come to the front of your picture. In our picture, we put one thickness of cork on the boy, two on the little girl and the white rabbit, and three on the rabbits in front and to the side of the girl. The branches each had small pieces of cork attached where they would not show. The boy was glued in first and we were careful to get his head so that it covered the oval shape just to the right of the lighthouse. Next we glued in the little girl and then the rabbit beside her. In order to make them look as though they were standing in grass, we added grasses and flowers in front of them. It was not necessary to use cork on these since we attached them to the girl and the rabbit with glue. Now the two front rabbits in the right corner were glued in and then the little shrubs and the rest of the grass. You may also attach some of your foreground to the glass which goes over your shadow box.

In working in a shadow box, one works with it lying flat on a table. Be sure to lift it occasionally, however, so that you are certain none of the cork backing will show.

You may use matchsticks, pieces of cardboard, or anything you think of, in place of the bits of cork used on our figures to bring them forward. In Plate 26, the scene in the Christmas tree ball was made by putting each figure, tree, etc., on eye-pins which were stuck into the styrofoam. Eye-pins are long pins with a loop (the eye) at one end which can be glued

Plate 26. *Christmas tree ball done by Rose Herber, St. Cloud, Minn., from cutouts from Christmas cards.*

to the object. They are obtainable in craft supply houses. Plates 25 and 26 are two of the type decoupage I call "for fun and for fancy." You can learn a lot by doing simple projects such as these. And if you will begin on such a project and do it carefully, you will soon reach the point where you not only want to try a more difficult and interesting piece of work but will be able to do it with confidence.

In doing any type Vue d'optique, it is important to keep in mind perspective. For example, in our little exercise, you know that the kitten on the little rise at top, left of the lighthouse, is much farther away from you than the mouse because of the size of the two animals. An excellent example of a complicated and beautifully executed Vue d'optique is that in Plate 27 by Patricia E. Nimocks. Notice the depth she has given the background building by shadows. The interior of the foreground building is enclosed in half a miniature matchbox which increases the three-dimensional feeling. If you plan a complicated shadow box, such as this one, go to a good instructor for your first project.

STUFFING AND MOLDING

The shadow box wastebasket in Plate 28 attained its three-dimensional quality through the stuffing and molding of the vase and the flowers. Plate 29 shows the materials needed to stuff and mold flowers, vases, figures, scrolls, etc. The flowers shown in this picture are not the same ones used in the wastebasket, but are for illustrative purposes only.

When all the cutouts are ready, prepare the stuffing from Kleenex and glue as follows. Tear two sheets of Kleenex into thin strips and place them in an electric blender, pushing the strips down around the blades lightly. Turn on the

Plate 27. Shadow box by Patricia E. Nimocks, Louisville, Ky.
The Venetian prints are colored in sunny yellows, shrimp, and
Mediterranean blue. The background is gold paper. The foreground building features an interior enclosed in half a miniature matchbox which increases the three-dimensional illusion.
Gold-paper braids are used to edge the frame and for the balus-
trade in the foreground.

Plate 28. *Wastebasket done by the author for Mrs. Johns McCulley, Sarasota, Fla. A hand-painted paper in shades of deep blue covers the outside of the basket. The background inside the shadow box is a deep rose velvet. The vase is delft blue with the cupid in white. Flowers are in shades of rose and pink. They were stuffed and molded. The base for the vase is made of cardboard covered with mother-of-pearl to resemble marble.*

*Plate 29. Materials and tools needed for stuffing and molding.
The dark flower on the left has a mixture of glue and Kleenex
in the center. The center flower shows how it looks when stuffed
and molded. The flower in lower center has been stuffed and
molded and then built up with the addition of extra petals. See
text.*

blender for a few seconds until you get a soft, fluffy substance. Now do two more sheets. By using only two sheets at
a time, your Kleenex strips will not wad. You will have to
learn to judge just how much fluff you need for a given
project but I find it well to do a whole box of the regular-
size Kleenex when I begin. What is not needed can be put in
a glass jar and kept for future use.

Use a water-soluble, clear-drying glue, such as Duratite, to
which you have added a quarter glycerin. Mix this with your
fluff. Do not mix large quantities. It is easy to do more when
you need it. The mixture should be pliable, but not runny.
Assume that you are stuffing the shaggy flower shown in Plate
28. Turn it over and put some of your mixture in the center.
Work this out toward the edges and turn the flower over on
a piece of wax paper. Now you can begin the molding. Work
for a natural effect. The dark flower to the left in Plate 28
shows the first step, and the middle flower shows the final
effect. The edges of the petals were left free of the mixture
so that they would look naturally fluffy. And even if you were
stuffing a number of tiny flowers or scrolls for a border on a
table, the edges should be left free of stuffing so that they can
be glued down tight before varnish is applied.

In molding, use your fingers or modeling tools similar to
those shown in Plate 29. The fat look in the center flower in
this plate was obtained by placing one tool at A and pressing
down to hold the flower at that point. Now place your second
tool at B and push toward A until you get the fatness you
want. The zinnia at the lower center was not only molded
but given additional petals which add to the natural look.
Such a flower would be used only in pictures. Care must be
used to get the petals tucked in so that just the outer edges
show. Otherwise the process is simply one of building up

layers of petals by gluing only the inner edges into the original stuffed flower.

As you finish each flower or other object, set it aside to dry. The drying time varies, depending on the humidity, but I find that most things will dry within five hours. The time may be speeded up by placing the figures in a warm oven. However, I do not recommend this to beginners since, no matter how much some of them are warned, they will get the oven too hot. The sun is an excellent dryer. When you put your figures in the sun, turn them face down with the stuffing toward the sun. Once dry, your stuffed objects will be hard enough to bounce.

Now let's go back to our wastebasket in Plate 28 and see exactly how it was put together. First I covered the box with dark blue wallpaper and then made a lining of rose-colored velvet (see Chapter 2 on linings). Next I colored and cut three sets of each flower, two sets of each leaf and the vase, and one butterfly. After all the cutting was done, I laid the vase on and placed some flowers and leaves in it. I realized that it was going to need more height than I had. At this point, I made the standard on which the vase rests by covering cardboard with mother-of-pearl (see Chapter 5). I cut a piece of cardboard the width and length I needed and folded it at each end. On top of this I glued another piece of cardboard. When the glue was completely dry, I covered with mother-of-pearl, cutting and fitting each piece and gluing them on. Now this was glued in at bottom center. The two lower roses hanging over the vase, the vase itself, and the carnation falling out of the vase were stuffed and molded as described above. The other flowers were given a three-dimensional look by using three cut-out flower heads for each flower. On top of the first was glued a small piece of cork and a second flower head was glued to this and also glued at the bottom where it joins the stem. The third flower head was glued on in the same manner. If you will look carefully at the tulip you will see that where it joins the stem, it was not glued on straight. This illustrates what I mean by gluing the flower head not only to the cork between each flower head but also to the bottom where it joins the stem. But glue it on straight. Do as I tell you and not as I do.

When the stuffed vase had dried, it did not satisfy me. I wanted the cupid to look as though it were raised. So I cut the cupid from the second vase I had colored and cut out and molded this separately; then I glued the stuffed cupid over the first vase. The carved effect I achieved was just what I wanted. Now the vase was glued on and the flowers, stems, and leaves glued in place. The butterfly was cut out inside and mother-of-pearl glued on back to show through the cutouts.

When the picture was finished and the glue dry, I put on the glass, which was cut to fit exactly. Gold-paper braid, painted a dull blue with a little gold showing through, finished the basket.

Part II
Today's Decoupage and Decoupeurs

Plate 30. Wall panel by Mrs. W. James Moore, Lowell, Mass. The background is celadon green. Each theme is from a different source, but all are original engravings except for the cascade of jasmine, which is from a copy of an old print. The cutouts are uncolored except for the jasmine which is pale blue with green leaves. The top is from an early map of Catalonia, 1762. See Ch. 5, p. 91.

Plate 31. Dressing table in the chinoiserie style by Mrs. Stephen L. French, South Swansea, Mass. The background is blue pompadour. The prints are all copies of Jean Pillement. The cartouches are in Venetian yellow. The carving was done by Mrs. French and is gold-leafed.

Plate 32. Back of table in Plate 31.

Plate 33. *Old metal envelope box, old metal scoop, and metal tool box by Alice Balterman, Cincinnati, Ohio. The envelope box is decorated with original black and white prints, the figures being cut out and superimposed to give a three-dimensional effect. These are good examples of "trompe l'oeil."*

Plate 34. *French provincial cabinet filled with miniature furniture and boxes from the collection of Mrs. Burt H. Payne,
Sarasota, Fla. Mrs. Payne used copies of a variety of 18-century
prints for her work.*

Plate 35. *Panel of an unfinished screen by Mrs. I. B. Swigart, Sarasota, Fla. The design is composed from some 30 different copies of 18th-century prints. Most of these are French, including Watteau, Boucher, and Pillement. The background is white and the prints are colored in lovely pastels with the wrought-iron effect in gold.*

Plate 36. *Small chest in the chinoiserie style by Mrs. Carl F. Sturhahn, Sarasota, Fla. The outside of the chest is a very dark, almost black, green with Pillement cutouts in deep yellows, rose and light green. The inside is painted avocado and decorated with Pillement flowers.*

Plate 37. Part of a Martha Washington sewing table done by the author. The table is natural mahogany and the cutouts, from copies of Boucher angel and French flower prints, are in pastels.

*Plate 38. China cabinet, courtesy Mr. George Skakel, Jr.,
Greenwich, Conn. The decoupage was done by Maybelle and
Hiram Manning for the late Mrs. George Skakel, Sr.*

Plate 39. *Chippendale tray done by Mrs. Lee Brown, Sarasota, Fla., for Mrs. E. L. Hersey. With the exception of the cheetah, which is an actual photograph of one brought back from Africa by Mrs. Hersey, the animals are cutouts from a print by Benson B. Moore. The background is black and the prints a greenish-brown. The border was designed from the print shown in Plate 6. It was colored in the same greenish-brown as the prints.*

Plate 40. *Bucket and two boxes by Bette Pearce, Greensboro, N. C. The butter bucket is stained brown and decorated with colorful cutouts from Hallmark cards. The card box on the right was decorated with parts of an early American birth certificate.*

Plate 41. Tray from modern French posters by a child who perfers to remain anonymous.

Plate 42. Three baskets and a box by Muriel W. Lane, Sarasota, Fla., for the St. Boniface Episcopal Church Bazaar. The decorations are cutouts from children's nature books and from wallpaper.

Plate 43. Italian commode by Mrs. Burt H. Payne, Sarasota, Fla. The background is ivory and the chinoiserie cutouts are in soft shades of rose-brown, green, and pastels.

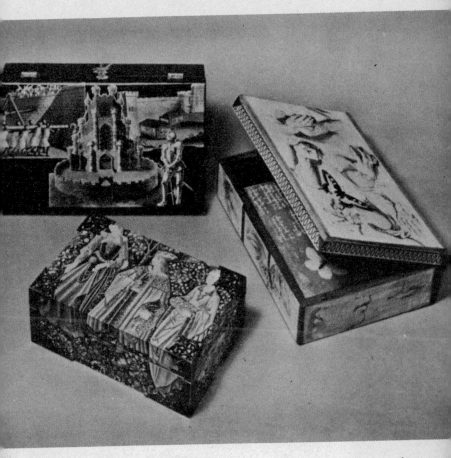

Plate 44. Three wood boxes by Alice Balterman, Cincinnati, Ohio. The box at top left is in the "trompe l'oeil" style. It is decorated with hand-colored prints of knights, castles, etc. The box to the right is done with cutouts from an 18th-century drawing instruction book. The inside is lined with reverse (negative) reproductions of Da Vinci's anatomical drawings and notes.

Plate 45. *Poodle bed by Mrs. Stephen L. French, South Swansea, Mass. The cutouts are from old French prints. Mrs. French reports that this bed is used by "Sweet Sue," a darling Harlequin toy poodle. She adds that, according to Hiram Manning, Boston, Mass., the bed is a copy of Marie Antoinette's poodle beds.*

Plate 46. *An old yellow crackle ceramic cigarette box by Mrs. W. James Moore of Lowell, Mass. The cutouts, which are from engravings of architectural details for the exteriors of buildings, are colored in deep reds and greens.*

Plate 47. Two pieces under glass by Patricia E. Nimocks and Mrs. David Halley, Louisville, Ky. The door push plate by Mrs. Halley is decorated with cutouts from Pillement prints in brilliant colors with a background of gold leaf.

Plate 48.   Shadow box executed by the author in the Maybelle
Manning Studio, Boston, Mass. The background is of velvet in a
shade of beige so light as to give the illusion of "no color." All
the flowers, cupids, scroll, etc., which are stuffed and molded
for a three-dimensional effect, are in two shades of blue. The
ferns are a yellow-green. See Chapter 5 for a discussion of working in shadow boxes.

Plate 49. *Tray by Mrs. William Almon Wood of New Canaan, Conn. The tray, which was painted antique white, has turned a soft old-yellow under varnish. The cutouts are from L'Illustration.*

Plate 51. *Two boxes by Mrs. Hiland Hall, New Canaan, Conn. The right-hand box, with cutouts from a Kate Greenaway book, is done in a shadow box with elevations (see Chapter 7).*

Plate 50. *Three metal trays by Alice Balterman, Cincinnati, Ohio. The oval tray is done with black and white prints and with photographs of sculptured heads of various historical periods. The lower tray, which is a good illustration of "trompe l'oeil," is done with assorted figures in color cut from reproductions and grouped to form a stage theme. The tray at the right uses an old theatre program, over which are superimposed figures from a 19th-century book.*

Plate 52. *Set of three tables by Mrs. Burt H. Payne, Sarasota, Fla. The background is a lovely warm beige and the cutouts, which are from Pillement prints, are in warm browns and bronzes.*

Plate 53. Oval wood box by Mrs. W. James Moore, Lowell, Mass. The box was first covered with linen and then gessoed but not painted (see Chapter 2). The cutouts, from Italian 16th-century prints, are in brilliant colors, the bodies being a violent deep green and the draperies red.

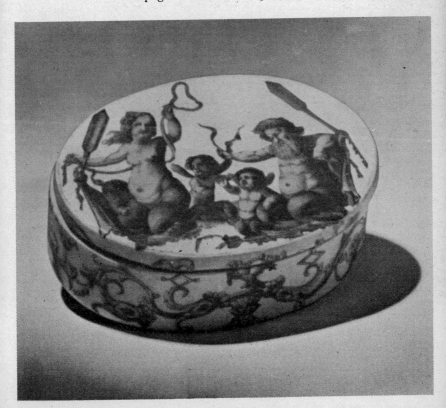

Plate 54. Tray and box by Bette Pearce, Greensboro, N. C. The tray is black with a gold edging. The design is from imported wrapping paper in shades of green and rust. The black box has a rich red trim. The design is from a bookmark from the Museum of Fine Arts, Boston, Mass.

Plate 55. *French ebony hand mirror by Mrs.
W. James Moore, Lowell, Mass. The mirror is
painted Venetian yellow and the cutouts, from
17th-century Italian engravings, are in soft grays
and blues.*

Plate 56. Metal wastebasket by Alice Balterman, Cincinnati, Ohio. Decorations are from a 17th-century print.

Plate 57. An antique English inlaid knife box by Mrs. W. James Moore, Lowell, Mass. The 18th-century box is walnut. The cutouts, in black and white, are from a book of armor (Italian 17-th century).

Plate 58.   Back of English knife box shown in Plate No. 57.

Plate 59. *Jewel box by Mrs. Burt H. Payne, Sarasota, Fla. The box is white with the design done in soft colors from copies of Boucher angels and old border prints.*

Plate 60. Box by Mrs. W. A. McCormick, New Canaan, Conn.
The box is white with animal cutouts in natural colors.

Plate 62. *Bristol egg by Mrs. W. James Moore, Lowell, Mass. The egg, which is painted yellow, is decorated with English pinks and green foliage. The wrought-iron base is enameled in the same colors. The egg and stand, which are old, are 13″ high.*

Plate 63. Lamp by Mrs. Alfred Hand, Washington, D. C. The lamp is decorated with cutouts from a hummingbird print in color. The background color is a soft yellow.

Plate 64. Box by Bette Pearce, Greensboro, N. C. This hand-made box is decorated with cutouts from drapery fabric in light-blue, dark blue, and rust.

Plate 65. Love seat and chair, courtesy Mrs. George Terrien, Greenwich, Conn. These pieces were decoupaged by Maybelle and Hiram Manning for the late Mrs. George Skakel, Sr.

Plate 66. Box done by Mrs. Burt Payne, Sarasota, Fla., from written instructions and materials from the Maybelle Manning Studio, Boston, Mass. According to the information furnished by the Mannings, the box is a copy of one presented to Williamsburg by Queen Elizabeth.

Plate 67. Cigarette box by Bette Pearce, Greensboro, N. C. The design was taken from a bookmark entitled "Dancing Hours," Fogg Art Museum, Harvard University. The background is Wedgwood blue and the trim is gold-paper braid painted white.

*Plate 68.   Tray by the author from copies of Pillement prints.
The background is deep rust and the cutouts are in soft greens
and yellows.*

Plate 69. Box by Mrs. Alfred Hand, Washington, D. C. The box is black and white with a brilliant red velvet lining. The cutouts are from Ladies' Amusement Book.

Plate 70. A pair of wall brackets by Mrs. W. James Moore, Lowell, Mass. The background is lapis lazuli blue and the cutouts are in pinks, yellows, pale blues, and greens.

Plate 71. Metal desk basket, cigarette case, and two boxes by Alice Balterman, Cincinnati, Ohio. The basket has a parcel post theme done in black and white with touches of red. The cigarette case has a mosaic effect built up from cutouts of paper, small sections of scenes, etc. The thin box in lower center is done from a stained-glass reproduction in brilliant colors. The box to the right is in black and white with a patriotic theme.

Plate 72. *French Provincial chest by Mrs. Stephen L. French South Swansea, Mass. The background is pompadour blue with Venetian yellow cartouches. The carving was done by Mrs French and gold-leafed. All the cutouts are from copies of Pille ment prints.*

Plate 74. French commode, courtesy Mrs. George Terrien, Greenwich, Conn. The decoupage was done by Maybelle and Hiram Manning for the late Mrs. George Skakel, Sr.

Plate 76. Chest by Mrs. William Almon Wood and Mrs. Hiland Hall, New Canaan. Lamp by Mrs. John Oldrin, Darien, Conn. The chest and box are done with cutouts from a book by Kate Greenaway. The lamp was done for Mrs. Oldrin's son with cutouts from his favorite book, Robert Lawson's Edward, Hoppy, and Joe.

Plate 77. Box done with prints from Ladies' Amusement Book
by Mrs. William Crawford, New Canaan, Conn.

Plate 78. Box by Mrs. Hiland Hall, New Canaan, Conn., with cutouts from illustrations from a book of Charles Dickens.

Plate 80. A tray by Mrs. Frank H. Boos, Grosse Pointe Farms, Mich. The tray is a handmade walnut one designed and executed by Mrs. Boos from Goya prints to resemble the work that Goya did as court painter of Spain. The colors are in rich reds, golds, yellows, and black.

*Plate 81. Dressing table and bench by Mrs. Frank H. Boos,
Grosse Pointe, Mich. These are delightful fantasies created by Mrs. Boos from many prints. The table shows a Japanese
prince on horseback coming to claim his bride-to-be from her
father, who is standing by. A priest is writing a marriage con-
tract on a scroll.*

Appendix

Notes on Decoupeurs and Decoupage Groups
Whose Photographs Appear in This Book.

The photographs throughout the book were collected from decoupeurs in many parts of the country. Although the list of contributors includes only a fraction of those doing decoupage, it represents a good cross section. The following notes on some of the groups and individuals may stimulate readers to form their own groups or to set up a studio where others may come and work.

The Sarasota group has been working together since 1958. Seven persons started with Dorothy Harrower in my Sarasota studio. Since then many of us have studied with Maybelle and Hiram Manning, Boston, and all of our present group have studied with me. Our work group, which meets once a week, is entitled "the clinic" by Mrs. Burt H. Payne, one of the original workers. There is no teaching in this group— its sole purpose is to do decoupage with other experienced workers. No one is invited to join who has not had a basic course. In winter, the group is augmented by visiting decoupeurs from many parts of the country. This gives us an opportunity to see what others are doing, to show them what we are doing, and to see each other's problems with new eyes. The give-and-take of such sessions is one of the most rewarding experiences in decoupage.

Among our group are Mrs. Burt H. Payne, Mrs. Carl F. Sturhahn, Mrs. Irving Swigart, Mrs. Lee Brown, and Mrs. Muriel Lane.

Mrs. Payne is the town's—and, I sometimes suspect, the nation's—most enthusiastic decoupeur. Not only has she done a magnificient collection of miniature furniture, but she has done everything else from boxes to large pieces of furniture. She never leaves for a summer vacation that she doesn't take with her dozens of prints which are colored and ready for cutting. When she gets home in the fall, she is ready with cutouts for all the projects she has laid out for the winter.

Mrs. Sturhahn has done decoupage for herself, for her children, for her grandchildren, for her great-grandchildren, and for her friends. One of our original group, her interest continues unabated and she always has time to discuss decoupage problems with others.

Mrs. Swigart's first love was flower arranging but today that has been pushed into the background by decoupage. Her knowledge of design, learned from flower arranging, is clearly apparent in her decoupage.

Wherever there is a studio of decoupage offering instruction and carrying decoupage supplies, groups spring up in the neighboring towns. In Boston, where the Mannings have taught for many years, there are groups in many of the suburbs as well as in Boston. And Maybelle and Hiram are such inspiring teachers and such delightful individuals that many of their first students are still going back to the studio for inspiration. One of these, Mrs. W. James Moore, Lowell, Massachusetts, is tremendously talented. In submitting photographs of her work, she wrote that all of them were done under the personal tutelage of the Mannings. Satisfied with nothing less than perfection, Mrs. Moore turns out only works of art. She is an indefatigable huntress, tracking down antiques and other unusual objects and finding prints to use for her cutouts in every conceivable place.

Mrs. Stephen L. French, South Swansea, Massachusetts, not only studied with the Mannings but has helped them from time to time in their teaching. In addition to decoupage, she also does hand carving, examples of which can be seen in her photographs.

Louisville, Kentucky, is a decoupage town. At Connoisseur Studio, Patricia E. Nimocks has taught many decoupeurs. Mrs. Nimocks discovered what decoupage was all about some eight years ago when she was restoring a Venetian secretary. It was so dark when she began on it that its decoration was almost invisible. After restoration, she found that the decoration had been done with paper cutouts. She immediately set about learning the art.

Through her interest in conserving works of art, Mrs. Nimocks learned many formulas and has developed and is developing new ones to fit specific needs. Her "Treasure Gold" is just what its name implies—a treasure to all who want to get a gold-leaf effect without the use of actual gold leaf. Examples of decoupage by Mrs. Nimocks and her students are included in our photographs. The students include Mrs. Fred Sheehan, Mrs. Richard Clark, and Mrs. David Halley.

In Greensboro, North Carolina, where Bette Pearce does the work of ten women rolled into one, there is a decoupage clinic once a week for the hundreds of women who come from miles away to bring their problems to an expert. Bette teaches at The Patio Studio in Greensboro. Her interest in decoupage is a natural one since she has worked at all types of crafts for years and has her own woodworking shop. Bette reports that she has a large proportion of men in her classes, many of whom come as skeptics but remain to cheer and to turn out excellent work. Enthusiasm in this North Carolina area is so great that some of the students dub themselves "decoupoors" because they spend all their time and money on their hobby.

Alice H. Balterman of Cincinnati, Ohio, became intrigued with decoupage as a means of using her many prints and pictures, which she has collected since her art school days. She wrote that she read about decoupage some eight years ago and developed her own style and technique through trial and error. As you will see from her photographs, Mrs. Balterman is a completely individualistic worker and a first-rate artist. She sells decoupage under her own name and under AHB Decoupages. But, as she pointed out, "Production is limited as each piece is individually hand-made and consequently is 'one of a kind.'"

A Connecticut group, taught and inspired by Mrs. William Almon Wood, New Canaan, is one of the finest groups in the country. Mrs. Wood first practiced decoupage in Detroit in the early 1950's. When she came to New Canaan in 1957 she joined the New Canaan Sewing Group whose chief purpose is to help finance the Visiting Nursing Association. A Spring Preview is scheduled each spring to show items which will be on sale in the fall at a one-day Christmas sale. Mrs. Wood

soon found herself teaching decoupage to some fifteen of the
sewing group and decoupage has become one of the most
popular tables at the Christmas sale. Meanwhile, Mrs. Wood
has taught in New Haven, Connecticut, Washington, D. C.,
and other cities. Photographs of the work of Mrs. Wood and
her students, including Mrs. John Oldrin, Mrs. Hiland Hall,
Mrs. W. A. McCormick, and Mrs. Wm. Crawford, are included.

Mrs. William F. Gillespie, Jr., began decoupage in the
Maybelle Manning Studio in Boston, Massachusetts. She has
done many magnificient pieces, including the 18th-century
screen shown in Part II. Mrs. Gillespie is a woman of many
talents and is now engaged in running a gourmet food shop
in Syracuse, New York, where her own specialties are
featured.

Mrs. Alfred Hand, Washington, D. C., teaches decoupage
to selected groups of students in that city. She has collected
many of her materials abroad and is an enthusiastic worker.

Some of the oldest decoupage groups in the country are
located in the Detroit, Michigan, area, including Grosse
Pointe, Grosse Pointe Farms, and Birmingham. Photographs
of the work of Mrs. Frank H. Boos, Grosse Pointe, show the
work of a master craftsman. Many decoupeurs in the area
work for the famous Christmas fair held each year in Grosse
Pointe for the benefit of the Grosse Pointe Memorial Church
(Presbyterian) and Christ Church (Episcopal). The profits
go to one church one year and to the other on alternate
years. In 1963, the decoupage table took in over $1,200.00.

Information on the well-known decoupeurs Maybelle and
Hiram Manning, Dorothy Harrower, and Carl Federer is
given in Chapter 1.

Since 1965 I have taught many people from all parts of the country, and some of them have become excellent teachers. Among them are Marge Billing of Boca Bazaar in Boca Raton, Fla.; Margaret Bennet of Roxboro, N.C.; and Dola Bice of Bartlesville, Okla.

Glossary

ASSEMBLAGE—A term adopted by William C. Seitz in his book *The Art of Assemblage* (see Bibliography) to include "all forms of composite art," including collage, montage, decoupage, etc.

BAROQUE—From the Portuguese meaning irregularly shaped pearl. The term was first used in the 17th and 18th centuries as a word of scorn to describe the overornate and heavy decorations in architecture, decorative art, etc., which came into vogue at that time. Today it is an historical term referring to the art style of the 17th and early 18th centuries as distinguished from the classical styles preceding it.

CADUCEUS (L)—A replica of a staff with two entwined snakes. The insignia bearing the caduceus symbolizes a physician.

CARTOUCHE (F)—An irregular, frequently scroll-like frame enclosing space for designs, inscriptions, etc. The word is used in decoupage to describe decorative designs which are usually oval or irregularly oval in shape.

CHINOISERIE (F)—An art style embodying Chinese motifs and designs. See Chapter 1.

COLLAGE (F)—A composition, usually within a frame, in which painting is combined with pasted-on objects, such as pieces of paper, string, shells, bits of wood, etc. A collage may also be done with no painting at all. See Chapter 1.

COUPER (F)—To cut.

DECALCOMANIA (F)—The process of transferring stamped-out pictures, designs, etc., to a surface. Also an item so decorated.

DECOUPAGE (F)—A term adopted in the 20th century to describe the art of decorating surfaces permanently with paper cutouts.

DECOUPEUR (F)—In decoupage, one who performs the art.

DECOUPURE (F)—A cutout. In the early 20th century, sometimes this term was used to denote decoupage.

JAPANNING—Lacquering. The term was used in 18th-century England to denote both the painted lacquer ware done in imitation of the Chinese and Japanese and the later art of decorating surfaces with paper cutouts. See Chapter 1.

LACCA CONTRAFACTA (It)—Simulated lacquer. The term is used in Italy today to describe the art of decoupage. See Chapter 1.

LACCA CONTRAFATTA (It)—See "Lacca Contrafacta."

LACCHE POVERO (It)—Poor man's lacquer. The term was used in 18th-century Italy to describe the art of decorating surfaces with paper cutouts. See Chapter 1.

LACQUE PAUVRE (F)—Poor man's lacquer. The term was used in 18th-century France to describe the art of decorating surfaces with paper cutouts. See Chapter 1.

L'ART "SCRIBAN" (F)—Literally, desk art. A term used in France both in the 18th century and today to describe what we term "decoupage."

MONTAGE (F)—A mounting. As an art term, the word was originally "photomontage," which was a 19th-century term for an arrangement of photographs or parts of photographs in such a way as to form an entirely new picture. Today the word is used to describe a composition, usually within a frame, which is made of various pictorial elements.

PAPIER-MÂCHÉ (F)—Literally, chewed-up or cut-up paper. Material for molding figures, flowers, animals, borders, etc., which is made from cut- or torn-up paper (usually newspaper) and glue. The material is very hard when dry.

RHUS VERNICIFERS (L)—A tree, indigenous to China, whose sap is used for Chinese and Japanese lacquers.

ROCOCO (F)—From the French "rocaille," meaning rock- or shell-work. *Rococo*, which is actually the last phase of *baroque*, came into being during the regency of the duc d'Orleans after the death of Louis XIV in 1715. The duc d'Orleans set the tone for a lighter, more fastidious, and more intimate art style. The style reached its height of originality under Louis XV and subsided soon after the accession of Louis XVI and Marie Antoinette.

SCRIBAN (*or Scribanne*) (F)—Desk. This word is seldom used to-day, having been superseded by the term "secrétaire."

TROMPE L'OEIL (F)—Literally, fooling the eye. In decoupage, the term is used to designate decorated surfaces on which flat cutouts are placed in such perspective that they give the illusion of three dimensions.

VERNIS MARTIN (F)—A varnish which bears the name of the five Martin brothers who first made it in 18th-century France. The term is also used to refer to 18th-century French lacquer ware.

VUE D'OPTIQUE (F)—Optical illusion. In decoupage, the term is used to designate three-dimensional designs in shadow boxes where the effect of space and vistas is achieved by use of elevations and perspective. See Chapter 7.

TOILES DE JOUY (F)—Drapery, upholstery, and other fabrics of cotton or linen which were printed in many gay and intricate patterns, including Chinoiserie, at Jouy, near Paris, in the 18th century. Copies of many of these are in use today.

Bibliography

Bates, Kenneth F., *Basic Design, Principles and Practice*. The World Book Publishing Co., New York, 1960.

Birren, Faber, *Monument to Color*. McFarlane Warde McFarlane, New York, 1938.

Brightbill, Dorothy Lambert, "Decoupage: Sudden Revival of an Old, Old Craft," *The American Home*, November 1958, p. 38.

Bustanoby, Jacques H., *Principles of Color and Color Mixing*. McGraw-Hill Publishing Co., New York, 1947.

Cennino D'Andrea Cennini, *The Craftsman's Handbook*. The Italian *Il Libro Dell' Arte*, translated by Daniel V. Thompson, Jr. Dover Publications, Inc., New York, 1933.

Crockett, Lucy Herndon, *Decoupage—The Pleasures and Perplexities of Decorating with Paper Motifs*. Printed for the author by Smyth County Print Co., Marion, Va.

Curtis, T. T., "The Story of Lacquer," *House and Garden*, April 1922, p. 41.

Duer, Caroline, "Decoupage—A Knowing Treatise on the Art of Cutouts." *House and Garden*, December 1949, p. 182.

Enabnit, Merlin, *Color with Palette, Knife, and Brush*. Walter T. Foster, Laguna Beach, Calif.

Encyclopaedia Britannica. Encyclopaedia Britannica, Inc., William Benton, Publisher, Chicago, Ill., 1963.

Bibliography

Germaine, Ira M., *Handbook of Color and How to Use It in Your Home*. Robert M. McBride and Co., New York, 1946.

Golding, John, *Cubism: A History and Analysis, 1907–1914*. George Wittenborn, Inc., New York, 1959.

Good Housekeeping
"Decoupage." il., January 1945, p. 120.
"She Decorates with Her Scissors." March 1942, p. 114.

Gough, M., "It's A Scissors and Paste Job When You Decorate with Decoupage," *House Beautiful*, March 1942, p 64.

Grotz, George, *The Furniture Doctor*. Doubleday & Co., Inc., Garden City, N.Y., 1962.

Guptil, Arthur L., *Water Color Painting, Step by Step*. Watson-Guptil Publication, Inc., New York, 1957.

Harrower, Dorothy, *Decoupage—A Limitless World in Decoration*. M. Barrows and Co., Inc., New York, 1958.

Honour, Hugh, *Chinoiserie—A Vision of Cathay*. E. P. Dutton and Co., New York, 1961.

House Beautiful
"Decoupage, Art of Decorating with Cut-outs, Again Returns to Fashion." June 1941, p. 52.

House and Garden
"Decoupage." October 1959, p. 158 ff.
"You Can Create Lasting Delight With Decoupage." February 1963, p. 118.

Knapp, Harriet E., *Design Approach to Crafts*. Prang Co. Publishers, New York, 1945, Division of The American Crayon Co., Sandusky, Ohio.

Lacquer, Oriental and Western, Ancient and Modern. Published by the Cooper Union Museum for the Arts of Decoration, 1951.

Ladies' Amusement or The Whole Art of Japanning Made Easy. Facsimile of the original published for Robert Sayer at the Golden Buck, Fleet Street, London, 1760, by the Ceramic Book Co., St. John's and Chepstow Rd., Newport, Monmouthshire, Wales, 1959.

Law, Margaret Lathrop, "Polish Paper Cutting." *House Beautiful*, February 1930, p. 118.

Lyon, Mary, *The Lively Art of Decoupage. Craft Horizons*, Summer 1950, p. 16.

Manning, Maybelle, "Decoupage: Hobby or Vice?" *American Home*, January 1949, p. 26.

Bibliography

Maybelle Manning Studios, *Decoupage—A Stylish Heritage from 18th Century France*. Printed privately and distributed from the Maybelle Manning Studios, Boston, Mass.

Oglesby, Catherine, *French Provincial Decorative Art*. Charles Scribners' Sons, New York, 1951.

Roche, M., "Le Décor 'Scriban.'" *Plaisir de France,* Noel 1960, p. 77.

Seitz, William C., *The Art of Assemblage.* The Museum of Modern Art, New York, in collaboration with the Dallas Museum for Contemporary Arts and the San Francisco Museum of Art, distributed by Doubleday and Co., Inc., Garden City, N.Y.

Stalker, John, *A Treatise of Japanning and Varnishing.* Oxford, England; printed for and sold by the author, living at the Golden-Ball in St. James Market, London, 1588.

Von Schmit, H., "Decoupage, Art of Decorating Furniture with Cutouts, Again Returns to Fashion." *House and Garden,* August 1939, p. 34.

Webster's Third International Dictionary, Unabridged, 1961. G. and C. Merriam Co., Springfield, Mass.

Weinberg, Louis, *Color in Everyday Life.* Moffat, Yard & Co., New York, 1922.

Whitaker, Frederick, NA, *Whitaker on Watercolor.* Reinhold Publishing Co., New York, 1963.

Index